AF556247

ACHIEVEMENT CORRELATES

Socio-Economic Status
Educational Aspirations
Adjustment
Educational Institutions

ACHIEVEMENT CORRELATES

Dr. Lavu Rathaiah
M.Sc., M.Ed., D.J., Ph.D.
Vignan Educational Institutions
Guntur - 522022

Dr. Digumarti Bhaskara Rao
M.Sc., M.A., M.A., M.Ed., Ph.D.
R.V.R. College of Education
Guntur - 522006

Editor
Mr. Paturi Koteswara Rao
M.Sc.
Vignan Vidyalayas
Hyderabad - Guntur - Visakhapatnam
Andhra Pradesh, India

Discovery Publishing House
NEW DELHI , INDIA

First Published – 1997

Reprinted – 2017

ISBN: 978-81-7141-385-0

Achievement Correlates

Published by:

DISCOVERY PUBLISHING HOUSE PVT. LTD.

4383/4B, Ansari Road Darya Ganj

New Delhi - 110 002 (India)

Phone: +91-11-23279245, 43596064-65

Fax: +91-11-23253475

E-mail: discoverypublishinghouse@gmail.com

sales@discoverypublishinggroup.com

web: www.discoverypublishinggroup.com

Printed at:

Infinity Imaging Systems

Delhi

Foreword

Intermediate is a crucial stage in a student's academic life. If one performed well at this class he will be on the high way to success.

But, many of our students are facing difficulties in their early college days due to content overload, adjustment problems, etc. Parents, educationists and government are worried about this problem.

Dr. L. Rathaiah and Dr. D. Bhaskara Rao investigated this aspect after observing different types of educational institutions at close quarters.

They have come up with appropriate recommendations. The present volume is the result of their efforts and bears the stamp of their rich experience. I commend this book to all individuals with a keen spirit of inquiry.

Prof. M. Malla Reddy
Vice-Chancellor
Osmania University
Hyderabad

Preface

Educational opportunities, though open to all, do not seem to engage to any reasonable extent the capacities of those who seek to avail themselves of them. An eternal question baffling parents, educators and planners is - why do students of demonstrated ability flop in their academic efforts at examinations? Academic under-achievement, more than academic failure, constitutes a grave problem as it amounts to wastage of manual and material resources which is construed as an irreparable loss to the society. This stimulated a number of researchers to undertake studies, like this one, on factors influencing academic achievement.

The researchers are interested in identifying the achievement position in Intermediate students studying in residential and non-residential junior colleges, besides its correlates. As the subjects are from Science and Mathematics groups, the achievement was high on the whole. Though the academic achievement was high, the residential college students fared well than their counter parts. This indicates that the residential system is playing a commendable role in academic performance.

The association between achievement and socio-economic status, achievement and educational aspirations, and achievement and adjustment was highly and positively significant; and this association was much high in residential colleges. Association between achievement and educational aspirations will be good, to many, in residential colleges as these subjects join these colleges with high educational aspirations. But, a shockening news to the criticisers of the residential system in the area of adjustment is - How these students adjusted better to the environment than their counter parts? The result of this study indicates that the residential system is developing a harmonious atmosphere in its campuses.

The parents, teachers and administrators should see that the socio-economic status, educational aspirations and adjustment of the students should be promoted to the desirable extent as these are positively associated with the achievement. The educational planners and administrators should also see that the facilities in educational institutions are improved to the optimum level to create a conducive teaching learning environment. The students should also aim according to their capacities, to avoid frustrations in future. This is the time for the students to involve devotedly in academic pursuits to settle in much credited professions.

The students, the parents, the teachers, the planners, the administrators, and the community should work hand in hand to create a society with all comforts to make the mankind live peacefully in luxuriousness.

Rathaiah Lavu
Bhaskara Rao Digumarti

Acknowledgements

We express our gratitude to Prof. M. Malla Reddy, Vice-Chancellor, Osmania University, Hyderabad for commenting on this book in his foreword. He is the guiding spirit behind this research.

We extend our thanks to our subjects for the courtesy of attending the instruments and to the heads of the colleges for the facilities they extended for data collection.

We will appreciate the researchers, teachers, planners and administrators if they use the results of this research in identifying the other correlates of achievement, in improving the teaching learning strategies, in developing appropriate curricular and co-curricular programmes, and in establishing the educational institutions with conducive teaching learning facilities.

Contents

Contents

INTRODUCTION

Of all the creations of Nature, human life is the most valuable one. The new born infant is a helpless human being and he grows in the protective and caring environment of the family. He is not only unaware of the social customs and traditions but is also devoid of any aim or objective. But as he grows older, he is influenced by the informal and formal agencies of education. In this way he develops his physical, mental and emotional self, and social feelings also develop in him gradually. By and by he is able to develop a sense of responsibility like his elders and solves the problems of life successfully. Education, in short, is able to instil in the child a sense of maturity and responsibility by bringing in him the desired changes according to his needs and demands of ever changing society, of which he is an integral part.

Education bestows upon the individual immense benefits. It guides him like an affectionate father, assists him honestly like a devoted wife, and serves him faithfully like a sincere servant. A well educated man is able to meet the conflicting challenges and tide over all the difficulties which confront him in day-to-day living. Not only this, education culturizes the individual and helps him in his needs all over the world. Thus education develops the individual like a flower which distributes its fragrance all over the environment. In this sense, education is that conducive process which leads a person out of darkness, poverty and misery by developing his individuality in all its aspects — mental, emotional, physical and social.

An individual, with an all-round development, becomes a responsible, dynamic, resourceful and enterprising citizen of strong, good, moral character and uses all his capacities to develop his own self, his society and his nation to the highest extent by contributing his best to national honour, glory, culture and civilization.

Education, on one hand, develops the full personality of an individual making him intelligent, learned, bold, courageous and strong with good character; on the other hand, it contributes to the growth and development of the society in particular and the nation at large. It is only through education that moral ideals and spiritual values, the aspirations of the nation and its cultural heritage are transferred from one generation to the other for preservation, purification and sublimation into higher and higher achievements. In other words, with the growth and development of the individual, the society also achieves higher levels of attainments. Thus, education is greatly essential for the growth and development of an individual as well as the society.

On the other hand, it has a social function also. The process of education is a social process or in other words child learns in a social environment. Through this process the mature members of the society pass on their own experiences, interests, purposes, attitudes and dispositions to the immature members of the society. The children would learn the mode of behaviour, formulate attitudes, and pick-up essential skills by seeing the elders, by mixing with them and by talking with them and hearing them.

In modern days the concept of 'education as a social function' has not changed, but the methods have changed. In the primitive days the society was not as complex as it is today and therefore it was then very simple for the society to transmit its experiences to the new generations. But, today's society being complex in its knowledge and skills, it cannot itself transmit all these directly to the fast rising new generation. Now there is a need for an organized formal institution to impart the essential knowledge and fundamental skills. Hence, the need for a school. But, the establishment of a school does not prelude the role of other educational agencies like home, temple, radio, press and several other influences of the environment. The school is only a selected and controlled environment.

The concept of formal education has a wider meaning and includes an educational set-up. At present, on the Indian educational scene, we follow the 10+2+3 pattern suggested by the Education Commission (1964-66). In these three stages the +2 stage is a critical one in many aspects as it possesses adolescents, forms the basis for entering professional courses, and acts as a stage between childhood and adulthood. The +2 students will be studying either in higher secondary schools or in junior colleges - residential or non-residential.

Education has become indispensable for every one. The machinery of government is inadequate to educate all. According to earlier targets, we had to educate all children by the time they attain 14 years of age. The year 1960 was thought of as the year for fulfilling the target. Even though three decades have elapsed since then we managed to educate nearly half of our total population, Here, one must not forget that private schools and colleges have the lion's share in promoting education.

On the old Indian educational scenario, the gurukulas (residential places of learning) played a very prominent role in educating the pupils or disciples. Later on, this system failed to cope up with the changes that occurred in the society and disappeared almost, to say frankly, and a new set-up of educational institutions came into existence and took deep roots. With the new system introduced and implemented by the British, many people got educated and obtained proficiency and efficiency in many fields of education and vocation.

Though the formal system of educational set-up has been providing education at its best to its non-boarders, it has certain disadvantages, which include - poor teacher taught relationship, improper discipline, under-achievement, irrelevant teaching and learning strategies, etc. At this hour, the importance of residential system offered by the 'gurukulas' in good olden days is identified as the best system to solve many problems in educating a child and to provide quality education through better and teaching learning strategies. This thought gave rise to many residential schools and colleges. The residential schools – such as Andhra Pradesh Residential Schools, Andhra Pradesh Social Welfare Residential Schools, Jawahar Navodaya Schools, Central Schools, and colleges - such as Andhra Pradesh Residential Junior Colleges, Andhra Pradesh Residential Degree Colleges, etc., have been established by both the state government and the central government. The residential institutions in Andhra Pradesh have excelled in academic achievement and allied areas and proved worthy.

On seeing the performance of the students of A.P. Residential Junior Colleges established in Andhra Pradesh in the early 1980s by the Government of Andhra Pradesh, the private managements started establishing residential junior colleges. At present, they out number the non-residential colleges - both government and private - in volume and strength.

Establishment of residential junior colleges in private sector, that too without any permission from the government, is not an amazing thing, but these private residential junior colleges are flourishing by leaps and bounds. For this the reasons are many and multidimensional. Let us discuss in detail the merits and limitations of both non-residential and residential junior colleges.

The Government of Andhra Pradesh has been spending to the tune of Rs. 200 crores on Intermediate education. The results are not in proportion to the expenditure incurred. Only 40 per cent of the students pass. In other words, two thirds of its expenditure is squandered away for nothing (Rathaiah and Bhaskara Rao, 1990). When private educational institutions are compared with those run by the government, the former are far better than the latter in respect of physical facilities, administration and staff. Above all they excel government colleges, in the matter of results.

Now private residential colleges have come up and these have been welcomed by those who want admission into professional colleges. In fact they have been weaning away a large number of students from government colleges. The government institutions and government aided private colleges have been unable to attract the cream of intermediate students. What are the features of private residential system that have been attractive to students ? To answer this, several other questions arise when we discuss the problem in detail (Bhaskara Rao, 1989).

Is the failure of private aided and government colleges a factor in the success of private residential college system ? Is the quality of teaching superior in private residential colleges to that of government and aided colleges ? Whether laboratory, library and other necessary physical facilities contribute to their success ? Is it the main aim of private residential system to earn more and more money ? Are these colleges getting good results because of malpractices ? Is there any real need for this rapid growth of residential colleges ? Are these colleges a burden to the government or to the society ?

Many think that the fast expansion of private colleges reflect the failure of the government in providing educational facilities to its people. But the reality is that education should not be monopolized by the government. Such monopoly involves colossal financial expenditure which is not proportionately matched by results. Even in the most advanced countries government will not undertake the entire responsibility of educating its public. Except in the socialist countries, government does not undertake the total responsibility of education.

When the private residential colleges grow, a large number of people who can afford to spend on education opt for these private residential colleges and those who cannot go to government institutions. With this the government can disburden itself, for, most of the financially sound students get their education without compelling the government to spend anything on them. Then, there will be a healthy competition between the two. So privatization of education brings healthy competition between the government and the private colleges, reduces the pressure on government institutions and offers chances to the students who can afford to have such education.

Time is precious and the two years a student spends in his intermediate course is more precious than any other period because that decides his future fate (Rathaiah and Bhaskara Rao 1990). In non-residential government and aided colleges, teachers and students stay together for only five to six hours a day. The rest of the 18 to 19 hours the student is left to his free will. Even if he wishes to clear his doubts, teachers are not available. With the result, the influence of the society is greater on him than on his counterpart in residential colleges.

A student, on the other hand, is given ample opportunity in residential colleges to pursue his education with single minded devotion and undivided attention, as the teachers are available at hand to clear his doubts. As the calibre of the students is very high, the teachers are always on the alert. As both teachers and students are committed to a goal and are led on the track of well-organized schedules there is no room for diversion either for the student or for the teacher. This is evident from the wonderful results they produce. Unprecedented rush to these private residential colleges is an illustrative proof of their good performance. The colleges speak for themselves by their results.

In respect of facilities — buildings, hostels, laboratories, play fields — the private residential colleges score points against the government managed or aided colleges. Teaching, learning, playing and extra-curricular activities are all in a single campus. They are not touched by the ripples and waves of academic restlessness of other colleges. They are the real, isolated islands of learning.

Students at the Intermediate level pass through adolescence (Bhaskara Rao, 1989). They need careful handling as they pass through physiological and psychological changes with their attendant problems. The big question is who will devote time and energy to their problems. Parents and the society are too busy to spare time for them. The teachers of government managed or aided colleges are deeply absorbed with their organizational problems. They are more often than not pegged down with their grievances. They, hence or otherwise, do not undertake the responsibility of the students.

The residential colleges are started for this specific purpose of attending to the needs of Intermediate students. As the teachers, students and authorities are under one roof any problem can be easily solved giving no room for dissatisfaction. These colleges forge emotional integration also among the students.

These residential colleges have been attracting students from all over the State. So the students are given a wonderful opportunity to mingle and develop their personalities (Rathaiah and Bhaskara Rao, 1990). While other colleges are the victims of local and non-local restraints, these residential colleges fully represent the culture of the state.

Finally, the residential system or the old gurukula system which we gave up long ago has come to stay. Residential colleges, may overcome the maladies that afflict the academic world to a certain extent.

With reference to this context, the present study entitled 'A comparative study of the achievement of Intermediate students studying in residential and non-residential junior colleges with special reference to its association with socio-economic status, educational aspirations and adjustment' has been taken up for a detailed study.

NEED OF THE STUDY

Life in general and for a student in particular has become highly competitive. Today there is no place for a mediocre student, there is limited room at the top that too only for the best. Almost all the attractive courses like medicine, agriculture, veterinary science, engineering, etc., have competitive tests for admission. A student with an ambition to secure admission to such courses should have a dedicated and methodical approach towards these examinations. And the basic subject material for these examinations is available only from intermediate course. So these two years of the intermediate course have become very crucial since these two years shape the entire future of a student.

A lot of importance is given to the colleges because that is where the student spends these two vital years of intermediate course, where he makes his future career. But, unfortunately, the situation in ordinary junior colleges, other than residential junior colleges, is not in any way encouraging. Innumerable maladies plague these temples of learning. The major problem in such colleges is regarding regularity. In almost all colleges, the studies, now-a-days, are interrupted by strikes, dharnas, bundhs, boycotts and so on resorted to one day by the students, another day by the teachers and on some other day by the non-teaching staff. With such frequent interruptions, the actual teaching period is going down drastically. Further, the concentration of the student is diverted by these disturbances.

It is also very important, in any competitive examination, that the student fares uniformly well in all subjects. Even if the student fares badly in one subject, the whole effort becomes waste. Now-a-days, a good combination of teachers is becoming a rarity in any college, because the cream of the educated youth, by and large choose, alternative vocations where they can make more money and consequently talented and efficient teachers have become a rare commodity. In many reputed colleges some of the teachers are outstanding where as others are mediocre, with the result the students fare very well in some subjects and only on an average scale and even very badly in others. So, there should be a perfect combination of teachers to impart uniformly good teaching in all subjects.

One more aspect in the place of intermediate education is parents. Most of the parents are busy with their own occupations and are unable to devote enough time to their children's education. They have the inclination but no time to do it. As a result most of them resort to sending their children to tutions and think that their responsibility is over. They fail to supervise their studies and fail to help them when they are lagging behind in some subject or other. To comfort such parents, there is the necessity of an institute which can provide good and well coordinated supervision for their children's studies. For such an effective supervision, the inclination on the part of the teacher and an attachment between the teacher and the taught are the necessary pre-requisites.

Further, the students of Intermediate course studying in junior colleges just enter the adolescent stage, which is a stage of stress and storm. In this period, they must be properly guided and counselled, otherwise there arises the problem of maladjustment. If the adolescents are once properly guided and aroused by right educational aspirations, they will excel in all aspects of life and education.

Government of Andhra Pradesh, for example, has been spending to the tune of Rs. 200 crores on Intermediate education. But the results are not in proportion to the expenditure incurred. Only 35 per cent of the students are successful, this too from the contribution of private colleges, particularly private residential junior colleges. In other words, two thirds of the expenditure is squandered away for nothing.

To solve the above discussed maladies of Intermediate education, a new system of education relevent to the contemporary needs of the society came into lime light with a name called 'residential' college/school. Here one can see the perfect combination of talented teachers, a 24 hour supervision with a personal touch and involvement, suitable guidance and counselling, right educational aspirations in students, healthy competition among the students, along with a perfect supervision and administration of administrators. Even admission into these residential junior colleges will be made mainly on merit basis and some private residential junior colleges keep in mind - an average student among meritorious students will be demoralized and will fare very badly even in future. Such minute concepts also creep into the minds of the administrators of the residential junior colleges.

The above arguments in favour of residential colleges and against non-residential junior colleges indicate that there should be a difference in the achievement of students studying in both kinds of these colleges. This study, hence, wants to identify the level of difference in the achievement of Intermediate students studying in residential - government and private - junior colleges and non-residential - government and private - junior colleges. It is also felt to identify the effect of socio-economic status, educational aspirations and adjustment on the achievement of the Intermediate students studying in these colleges.

OBJECTIVES OF THE STUDY

The following objectives were framed for the present research.

1. To compare the achievement of the Intermediate students of residential and non-residential junior colleges.

2. To find out the relationship between achievement and socio-economic status of Intermediate students.

3. To find out the relationship between achievement and educational aspirations of Intermediate students.

4. To find out the relationship between achievement and adjustment of Intermediate students.

5. To compare the association of achievement with socio-economic status, educational aspirations and adjustment of Intermediate students.

SCOPE OF THE STUDY

One of the most important outcomes of any educational set-up is achievement of the students. Depending on the level of achievement individuals are characterised as high-achievers, average-achievers and low-achievers. Many studies indicate that the academic achievement is dependent on variables like school/college set-up and its organization, socio-economic status of students, educational aspirations, well-adjusted behaviour, etc. Besides these the personal characters, vocational aspirations, creativity, intelligence, attitude, values, etc. , also influence it. But, socio-economic status, aspirations and adjustment play a major role. Hence this study is confined only to identify the relationship of achievement with socio-economic status, educational aspirations and adjustment of senior Intermediate students studying in junior colleges.

The major aspect of this study is to identify whether there is any difference in the achievement of the sample studying in residential and non-residential junior colleges. This is selected because the students studying in residential junior colleges, particularly in private residential colleges, are securing very high achievement and even getting state ranks in the Intermediate public examinations. With this aim, the present study is confined to the students of junior colleges, private and government and residential and non-residential.

This study does not consider the intervening variables like personality, creativity, motivation, intelligence, medium of instruction, and locality of the junior colleges.

With the above discussion the investigators interest is to say that the scope of this study is confined to the achievement of the senior Intermediate students studying in residential and non-residential junior colleges with special reference to its association with socio-economic status, educational aspirations and adjustment.

IMPORTANCE OF THE STUDY

Academic achievement is of paramount importance in the present socio-economic and cultural contexts. Obviously, at +2 stage, great emphasis is placed on achievement right from the beginning. This stage has its own systematic hierarchy which is largely based on achievement and performance as this stage is a channel to enter professional courses. So the junior colleges tend to emphasize achievement, which facilitates, among other things, to become professionals such as doctors, engineers, lawyers, chartered accounts and so on. The junior colleges perform the function of selection and differentiation among students on the basis of their scholastic and other attainments and open out avenues for advancement, again, primarily in terms of achievement. A considerable number of students from +2 stage studying in junior colleges also go to other institutions of higher learning.

The effectiveness of any educational system is gauged to the extent the students involved in the system achieve, whether it be in cognitive, conative or psychomotor domain. In general terms achievement refers to the scholastic or academic achievement on the student at the end of an educational programme. To maximize the achievement within a given set-up is, therefore, the goal of every educationist. Research has come to our aid by looking into what variables - personal, home, college, teacher, etc. - promote achievement and what are deterrents to it. It has been thus indicated that a good number of variables, such as personality characteristics of the learners, the socio-economic status from which they hail, the educational aspirations, the organizational climate of the institution, etc., to mention a few, influence achievement in varying degrees.

Heads of institutions, curriculum planners, teachers and others who are involved in the task of helping students to achieve better, would like to have a knowledge of the extent of the influence these correlates exert on achievement. Further, a synoptic view of the researches done would be of utmost importance to the educational researcher to enable him to explore greater depths in this, rather important area of achievement (Anand and Padma, 1989).

Behind these arguments is the assumption that the students will be benefitted by attaining excellence in academic achievement. The people associated with the achievement of college students will look into the flaws and merits of the achievement and take necessary steps to enhance the academic achievement.

The achievement of the students studying in residential junior colleges is better than that of the students of non-residential junior colleges. The percentage of passes is also very high in residential colleges (Bhaskara Rao, 1989). 'Why is there this disparity in these two types of junior colleges?' is the present day question of many people. The right answer includes many factors - quality teaching, well furnished labs, good libraries, conducive and competitive learning atmosphere, better teacher taught interaction, good supervision, timely administrative decisions, and so on (Rathaiah and Bhaskara Rao, 1990). Above these, the student's socio-economic status, educational aspirations, adjustment and personality play their legitimate role in achieving excellency in examinations. If we identify the factors concerned with the high achievement available in residential junior colleges, we can extend these factors to non-residential junior colleges to offer benefits to the students studying in these colleges.

Recent years have witnessed increasing public concern for the plight of the socially disadvantaged. Psychologists, long back interested in possible differences between individuals of varied social and economic backgrounds, have played a significant role in translating this concern into practical knowledge. Developmentalists have particular interest in trying to understand the relationship between development and factors unique to the disadvantaged. Many studies are confined to the effects of socio-economic status.

Since the society in India, as elsewhere, consists of different classes, it is but natural for the researchers to think of the extent to which home conditions influence the scholastic achievement of children. These home conditions, which are generally known as the socio-economic status, may be further sub-divided as parent's occupation and education, family income, family possession, and social participation. Researchers generally include socio economic status as one of the variables in their studies. The present study is considering the relationship between socio-economic status and achievement. After identifying the relationship between achievement and socio-economic status of the students, through this study, researchers shall explore factors that presumably are relevant to the development of socio-economically disadvantaged.

Aspiration is a longing for what is above, with advancement as its goal. It emphasizes the desire to improve or to rise above one's present status. An individual's aspiration level represents him not only as he is at any particular moment, but also as he would like to be at some point in the future. It is also a measure of his intentional disposition, an important element of his long range behaviour. The educational aspirations help a student to achieve them. For this he has to work hard, understand well, and apply perfectly. Previous studies indicate that there is a positive relationship between aspirations, vocational and educational, and achievement. Hence this study intends to know the relationship between educational aspirations and achievement.

Every human being seeks adjustment to various situations. He constantly makes efforts to adjust himself to his surroundings because a wholesome adjustment is essential for leading a happy life and gaining satisfaction. Satisfactory adjustment is characterised by behaviour which is both adaptive and constructive. Adjustment is the outcome of the individual's attempts to deal with stress and meet his needs: also, his efforts to maintain harmonious relationships with the environment (Coleman, 1969). Smith states that 'a good adjustment is one which is both realistic and satisfying. At least in the long run, it reduces to a minimum the frustrations, the tensions and the anxieties which a person must endure' (Rastogi, 1983).

There will be characteristic emotional disturbances in each stage of life which, although, subject to differential diagnosis, are determined by the life tasks of that stage of life and are most easily ameliorated during the very period of their emergence. In a school or a college situation most students will meet problems in some area of school or college life or other. The word problem is used here to refer to a situation to which one needs to make some sort of adjustment, i.e., rectification of earlier ways of dealing with it for maximum satisfaction. We prefer to call this kind of adjustment as academic adjustment, which would be a student's adjustment to his curriculum, his expressed satisfaction with the college routine in general and with his chosen curriculum in particular. Academic adjustment has often been defined as the adjustment of the student as measured through his scholastic success, that is, a well adjusted student is thought to be one who obtains high scholastic grades (Narayana Rao, 1990). Here, through this study, the relationship between achievement and adjustment can be identified.

EDUCATIONAL IMPLICATIONS

The major educational implications of the present study are -

1. The factors involve in high achievement will be extended to other achievement groups, and simultaneously the causes for middle or low achievement, if exist, can be rectified.

2. If there exists any difference in the achievement of the students studying in residential and non-residential junior colleges, suitable measures can be offered to avoid the difference in achievement.

3. The socio-economic status, one of the correlates of achievement, can be improved or at least its effect nullified if found it's positive influence on achievement.

4. Educational aspirations, the future goals of life, may be suitably modified depending on their aspirations.

5. Adjustment, the prime requisite of any living organism, can be improved through proper guidance and counselling if found unusual in the sample.

6. The relationship, positive or negative, of achievement with socio-economic status, educational aspirations and adjustment may help the educators and administrators for taking up necessary decisions to help the students.

RELATED RESEARCH

Any worthwhile research study in any field of knowledge requires an adequate familiarity with the work which has already been done in the same area. A summary of the writings of recognized authorities and of previous research provides evidence that the research is familiar with what is already known and what is still unknown and untested. Since effective research is based upon past knowledge, this step helps to eliminate the duplication of what has been done, and provides useful hypotheses and helpful suggestions for significant investigation (Best, 1982).

Citing studies that show substantial agreement and those that seem to present conflicting conclusions help to sharpen and define understanding of existing knowledge in the problem area, provides a background for the research project, and makes the investigator aware of the status of the issue. Parading a long list of annotated studies relating to the problem is ineffective and inappropriate. Only those studies that are plainly relevant, competently executed, and clearly reported should be included.

In searching related literature, the researcher should note certain important elements. They include - 1. Reports of closely related studies that have been investigated. 2. Design of the study, including procedures employed, and data-gathering instruments used, 3. Populations that were sampled and sampling methods employed, 4. Variables that were defined, 5. Extraneous variables that could have affected the findings, 6. Faults that could have been avoided, and 7. Recommendations for further research.

The search for related literature is a time consuming process, even though it is necessary, as earlier stated, for a good research work. Hence this chapter, Review of Related Literature, is meant for the study of achievement correlates such as, socio-economic status, educational aspirations, adjustment and the characteristics of educational institutions.

ACADEMIC ACHIEVEMENT

Education plays a vital role in building a society. A modern society cannot achieve its aims of economic growth, technical development and cultural advancement without fully harnessing the talents of its citizens. Educationists thus strive to develop fully the intellectual potential of the students and make efforts to see that their potentialities are fully realized and channelized for the benefit of the individuals and that of the society.

Educational opportunities, though open to all, do not seem to engage to any reasonable extent the capacities of those who seek to avail them of. An eternal question baffling parents, educators and national planners is : why do students of demonstrated ability flop in their academic efforts at school or college examinations? Academic under-achievement, more than academic failure, constitutes a grave problem as it amounts to wastage of human resources which is construed as an irreparable loss to the society, which, a developing country like ours can ill afford. This stimulated a number of researchers to undertake studies, like the present study, on factors influencing achievement, a review of which is presented here under.

The concepts of over-achievement and under-achievement, logically speaking, are meaningful in relation to some expected level of performance. Theoretically, if one's performance is superior to the expected standard of performance then one may be regarded as over-achiever, whereas when one's performance is inferior then one may be regarded as under-achiever.

Scientists like Stanley, Ross, Frumar and Frazen feel that the phenomenon of over-achievement is, logically, spurious and meaningless since, according to them, no one can operate above the level of one's potential ability, from which most often, the standard of expected performance is derived. However, they assert that under-achievement is the indication level of full expression of one's potential ability. On accepting the theoritical definition of the concept of under-achievement which stresses that under-achievement is meaningful in relation to one's actual performance that may be adjudged, we are justified to ask as to from which level the expected performance comes.

Broadly speaking, there are two ways open for answering the question regarding the standard of expected performance. Either, the standard of expected performance may be subjective, or it may be objective. The subjective standard of expected performance may further be classified into two categories. In one type of the subjective standard of expected performance, the individual himself determines the standard of performance; whereas in the second type of subjective standard, the expected standards of performance is stipulated by the person who is operating as a 'significant-other' (parent or teacher) in one's process of socialization. We all know that the subjective standard of performance determined by significant others are so much subjective and irrational that they are rarely attainable. How-so-ever hard a student may try it is not possible to satisfy one's parents or teachers through his achievement.

Psychologically speaking, the subjective standard of expected performance, irrespective of the fact, whether it is arising from within or it is imposed by the parents or teachers from outside, is representing man's hopes and aspirations which are endless.

One more type of the subjective standard of expected performance is representing aspirations and hopes of one's spiritual leader or hero. Such a standard of expected performance is most often unrealizable and may be termed as the ideal standard of expected performance.

The expected standard of performance which comes from within the individual, is the outcome of his own aspirations and satisfactions related to his achievements. Previous experiences of success result in guiding a person for raising his level of expectation. Some individuals may be satisfied with the previous achievement while others may want to settle for higher grades. They are often eager to learn more, confident to do it and ambitious to achieve more.

Taylor (1964) states that the value the student places upon his own worth effects his academic achievement. Very low level of expectation tends to make a pupil accept very low standard of achievement, very high expectations lead to discouragement and diminished effort because he feels he cannot live upto what is required of him. To be practical, the level of expectation needs to be geared to suit each individual capability.

Many changes are being witnessed in organization, curricula, teaching strategies, etc. It is pertinent to seek systematic and up-to-date information on the significant correlates of a student achievement. It is also appropriate, in this context, to consider factors affecting the academic achievement such as the student's socio-economic background, educational aspirations, adjustment, etc., etc. These factors are of utmost, theoretical and practical, importance in developing curricula, and designing educational programmes to suit the needs of students with varied backgrounds. Further, the study of these factors assumes special significance in view of their implications in respect of day-to-day curriculum planning on the part of the classroom teachers. Studies on the correlates of achievement, thus, need to be thoroughly examined with a view to deriving maximum benefit from their findings for improved curricular development, efficient teaching, and better academic achievement.

ACHIEVEMENT AND SOCIO-ECONOMIC STATUS

At a time of lively appraisal of educational development, when many changes are being witnessed in organisation, curricula and teaching techniques, it is pertinent to seek systematic and up-to-date information on the significant correlates of achievement. It is appropriate, in this context, to consider at once the factors affecting academic achievement such as the student's socio-economic background, personality traits, study habits, attitudes, medium of instruction and so on. As this study intends to identify the relationship between achievement and socio-economic status of students, let us look into the findings of the previous studies in this area.

Clark (1927) found that students whose parents had college education ranked higher in scholarship. Shuttleworth (1927) reported that the low-achieving group of students had strict religious home training.

Bear (1928) found that parental occupation was related to academic success. He reported that sons of farmers and businessmen ranked low in scholarship in comparison with those of artisans, salesmen and so on.

Austin (1964) found very high relationship between the tendency to drop out of college and parents' education and father's occupation. Sinha (1970), and Wig and Nagpal (1970) found that low achievers represented more in occupational category-agricultural or business.

Griffits (1926) found a close relationship between school grades and family size. Children from small families were found superior in school grades.

Havighurst (1964) contrasted achievement test performance of middle-class and lower-class children in 21 Chicago school districts. He found that 6th grade students in the seven districts with the highest average socio-economic status ranged from grade level to one year above grade level in reading and mathematics tests; in the seven lowest socio-economic status districts, the scores clustered around one year below grade level.

Mishra, Das and Padhi (1960) reported a correlation of 0.59 between home environment and school achievement whereas correlation of 0.31 between intelligence test scores and school achievement.

Menon (1973) found over-achievement and under-achievement are highly influenced by socio-economic status. Anand (1973) established relationship between socio-economic status and academic achievement even when the influence of intelligence of non-verbal and verbal type was partialled out. He also found that the impact of socio-economic environment was found to influence mental abilities and academic achievement.

Abraham (1974) found achievement level in English is associated with socio-economic status and Basavayya (1974) observed that overall language achievement is influenced by the parental occupation and education.

A study on difficulties in learning English by Dewal (1974) revealed that effective teaching and learning are hampered by poor socio-economic background.

Bhaduri (1971) observed that the over-achievers showed higher scores in study habits, attitude to school, and religious-cultural background; the under-achievers on the contrary, tended to have a higher socio-economic status, a more congenial home condition and more of leisure time activities.

Lalithamma (1975) found that the achievement in mathematics was positively related to intelligence, study habits, interest in mathematics and socio-economic status. Correlation between socio-economic status and academic achievement as computed by Chandra (1975) was reported as positive and is supported by Homchandhuri (1980).

Satyanandam (1969) highlighted two sub-aspects of socio-economic status, viz., educational level of parents and economic status of parents. According to him, the children of graduate parents performed far better than the children of matriculate parents.

Children of upper and lower, upper and middle economic strata only differed significantly on the variable of achievement (Anand and Padma, 1987). Chatterji, Mukherjee and Banerjee (1971) also found that parent's education level was directly related to the achievement of their children.

Khanna (1980) observed that the academic achievement of the children of educated parents, illiterate parents, and educated mothers was significantly correlated with the socio-economic status of the family. Menon (1972) also noticed that higher occupational and educational level of father, educational level of mother, family income and parental attention were related to high achievement.

Ojha (1979) concluded that higher the socio-economic status the better would be the academic achievement at high school level. Parental education, occupation, and income were also related with the educational achievement of both rural and urban boys of 9th class.

Choudhari (1975) expressed an opinion based on research that bright children normally came from families where parents having a higher level of education, were mostly engaged in professions requiring general knowledge, and had more income than the parents of dull students. In Goswami's (1978) study also the scholastic achievement correlated highly with socio-economic status.

Goswami (1982) found a significant relationship between socio-economic status and reading interests and also between reading interests and academic achievement.

Jain (1981) states that the socio-economic level of the parents had a great impact on the pupil's achievement in

Gujarati language, social studies, science and mathematics. The pupils belonging to the upper socio-economic status achieved better than the pupils whose parents belonged to the middle and lower socio-economic levels, while the pupils from the middle socio-economic levels scored better than those with lower socio-economic status of the parents, in all the subjects. Academic achievement (Tripathi) had a high positive correlation with socio-economic status.

Family background factors of college students, according to Siddiqui (1979), had positive relationship with the academic achievement of the students when the intelligence factor was held constant. Somasundaram observed that the variables which discriminated between the unselected groups of normal and under-achievers were social standards, introversion and family relations.

Griffits (1926) observed that within the family the older and the younger children tended to perform about equally well scholastically. Gupta (1982) found that birth order and the father's profession influenced the reading ability (in Hindi) of children studying in classes III and IV.

Chatterji, et. al. (1971) concluded that the family size and the number of siblings were inversely related, especially in low intellectual level. Dave and Dave (1971) observed that the size of the family was not related to the academic achievement.

Dave and Dave (1971) noticed that a higher percentage of rank students belonged to homes having higher parental income, occupation and education, whereas a higher percentage of failed students belonged to homes having lower parental income, occupation and education.

In the study of Dhami (1974) the relationship between socio-economic status and academic achievement, though statistically significant, was not very high. Socio-economic status was moderately correlated with achievement in the study of Srivastava (1980). Sinha (1970) also observed only small differences on their parent's education and father's education. The socio-economic status of the pupils' parents was not significantly related to scholastic performance at Class VIII and Class IX but at Class X the pupils hailing from homes with higher socio-economic status performed better (Reddy, 1981).

Nemzek (1940) reported that education of parents and their profession have no influence over the academic success of their children. But for the high ability group, children of servicemen excelled the children of businessmen, and the trend was reversed for the average and low intellectual groups (Chatterji , Mukherjee and Banerjee).

Salunke (1979) found no relationship between socio-economic status and achievement. Bhat and Indiresan (1981) failed to draw definite conclusions regarding the differential performance of students belonging to different socio-economic backgrounds as the sample consisted mainly of students belonging to the backward class and low-income group.

Chatterji, Mukherjee and Banerjee (1971) concluded that the economic conditions of the family seemed to have no effect upon the scholastic achievement in all the intellectual ability groups. They also found that father's occupation was not consistently related to children's achievement. Desai (1979) observed no relationship between socio-economic status and achievement.

Socio-economic variables related students determined selection but were not relevant to subsequent academic performance (Nagpal, 1979).

Most of the studies in this category have attempted at replicating earlier studies taking different samples and by including different curricular subjects at various levels. We can't find a suitable research conducted taking samples from both residential and non-residential junior colleges which is a necessity to identify the association of achievement and socio-economic status in this sample.

ACHIEVEMENT AND EDUCATIONAL ASPIRATIONS

Aspiration is a natural phenomenon of human life, and educational aspiration is no exception. Level of aspiration, the level of future performance in a task which an individual acts for himself knowing his past performance, is considered to play a significant role in scholastic achievement. Some psychologists define the level of aspiration as the level of future performance in a familiar task which an individual expects to achieve knowing his level of past performance in that task. On other occasion Mathis, Cotton and Sechrest (1970) opined that the level of aspiration is the degree of performance a person expects of himself in a specific situation.

Lewin (1926) assumed that the relation of the level of aspiration to the level of past performance at any time depends primarily on the relative strength of the following needs - 1. the need to keep the level of aspiration as high as possible, regardless of the level of performance, 2. the need to make the level of aspiration approximate the level of future performance as close as possible, and 3. the need to avoid failure, where failure is defined as a level of performance below the level of aspiration, regardless of its absolute goodness and this need tends to drive the level of aspiration below the level of past performance.

It seems probable that the relative strength of these needs depends on the environmental factors but also on the personal factors of an individual. The person who habitually keeps his feet on the ground would be expected to keep his level of aspiration close to his level of past performance, while he whose head is in the clouds would keep his level of aspiration soaring high in any situation. A cautious individual would tend, as a rule, to keep his level of aspiration below his level of past performance and the ambitious person would typically set his level of aspiration high and persist high until he has raised his level of performance to meet it.

A mild degree of continued dissatisfaction is essential for providing motivation to an individual for continuously improving upon his past performances. If a state of complete satisfaction is arrived at, the process of further progress of the individual might come to a standstill. Therefore, for bettering the past achievement, a moderate degree of positive discrepancy between the level of the achieved and the level of the aspired is essential.

Level of aspiration is generally raised when performance equals the level of aspiration and lowered when performance falls below the level of aspiration. Jucknat (1937) studied the reaction of subjects to attainment or non-attainment of their levels of aspiration and found that stronger the feeling of success the greater is the tendency to raise the level of aspiration and that the tendency to lower the aspiration is greater with a strong feeling of failure. A commonly observed tendency of subjects is to maintain a moderate positive goal discrepancy.

Lewin (1944) reported that nearly all individuals of western culture, when first exposed to a level of aspiration situation, gave initially a level of aspiration which is above the previous performance score, and under most conditions tend to keep the goal discrepancy positive.

Festinger (1942) observed that after an attainment of the level of aspiration there was 51% rise, 41% staying on the same level, and 8% lowering of the level of aspiration. After a non-attainment of the level of aspiration, it was raised in 7% cases, stayed at the same level in 29% cases and lowered in 64% cases.

Menon (1972) found that job aspiration, educational aspiration and general ambition were strongly associated with high achievement, particularly in girls.

There are a few typical cases of equal importance. Sears (1940) observed that children with a past history of success showed very little variability in aspiration. Most of them maintained the typical small positive goal discrepancy. Children with past history of failure showed a much higher goal discrepancy and variability. Some had very high positive goal discrepancies, they set their level of aspiration very much above their immediate past performance. Similar patterns of aspiration have been observed in later clinical studies of the level of aspiration.

Studies of Gould and Kaplan (1940), Sears (1940), Holt (1942), Schultz and Ricciuti (1954) found no relationship between scholastic achievement and level of aspiration. Sharma (1979) also found that the level of aspiration did not influence academic achievement.

Muthayya (1962) concluded that high achievers and low achievers in scholastic do not significantly differ in aspiration level. Radha (1985) found that the level of aspiration has not been found to have significant bearing on academic achievement.

Gates and Jersild (1948) have stated that the level of aspiration is closely related to success and failure in college and that it may represent a goal or desire to improve the performance. Lowel and Atkinson (1953) reported a positive but low and not significant relationship between the level of aspiration and achievement motive among high and low achievers.

Kuppuswamy (1974) informed that the achievement in school is closely related to the level of aspiration. Shukla (1973) observed that the level of aspiration determines the limits of academic achievement to some extent. Hussain (1977) concluded that the academic performance of the group showing moderate goal discrepancy was better than that of the groups showing either high or low goal discrepancy, implying a curvilinear relationship between the level of aspiration and academic performance.

Bryan and Locke (1967) concluded that academic performance can be increased by suggesting what level a person should aspire for. Sears (1940) and Rotter (1943) have found that groups with a history of poor academic achievement had higher average goal discrepancy scores than groups with a history of high achievement.

Ramkumar (1972) observed a strong association between achievement and goal discrepancy and pointed out that achievement is higher with a decline in goal discrepancy scores.

With the above review of the available related research, one does not come across many research reports on the level of aspiration in relation to academic achievement. Some of the researchers have found no relationship between the level of aspiration and scholastic achievement, whereas some have found them to be positively related. As some researchers have reported, there seems to exist a negative relationship between achievement and the level of aspiration. None of the researchers reported above studied the relationship between the level of educational aspiration and achievement at +2 level, which is a crucial stage in the educational system.

ACHIEVEMENT AND ADJUSTMENT

Anywhere in the world, parents and teachers are concerned about the kind of adjustments children make. To them, the child's popularity or lack of it is so important that they do everything within their power to help the child to be socially acceptable member of the peer group.

Most parents realize that there is a close relationship between a child's adjustments and success and happiness in childhood as well as in later life. To ensure that their children will make good adjustments, they provide them with opportunities to have social contacts with other peers, and try to motivate them to be socially active, hoping that this will lead to good adjustments, social, home, health, emotional and so on.

Further more, some parents believe that a child who makes good adjustment will be laying the foundations for success in adult life. If the child is well accepted by peers, it will result in behaviour patterns and attitudes that will lead to a successful marriage and will be a stepping-stone to success in the vocational world, which will lead to upward social mobility.

Teachers are concerned about the social adjustments of their students because they know that well-accepted students are far more likely to do work in keeping with their capacities than those who are rejected or ignored by their classmates. Further more, they are less disruptive in the classroom and far less likely to become truants and dropouts than those who make poor adjustments.

Concern about the student's adjustments on the part of parents and teachers is justified for two reasons - First, patterns of behaviour and attitudes, formed early, tend to persist. Children who make good adjustment in the first grade, for example, are far more likely to make good adjustment when they reach high school or college than are children who make poor adjustment during first years of schooling. This, of course, does not mean that children who make a poor start will not improve their adjustment as they grow older. But doing so will be a long and difficult task and the chances are far less unless it better foundations had been laid during the pre-school and early school years. Second, the kind of adjustments children make leaves its marks on their self-concepts. This like-wise, contributes to the persistence of the pattern of adjustment. Children, for example, who make poor social adjustments are unhappy and learn to dislike others. As a result, they often develop into self-centered, introverted, unsocial, or even anti-social individuals whose adult happiness and successes are seriously jeopardized.

Stromswold and Wren (1948) feel that a well-adjusted student in school / college exhibits his intrinsic interest in the subject. Matter of study, positive attitude towards the requirements of curriculum, stability of goals, balanced emotional life, ability to concentrate for a reasonable length of time and ability to enjoy life in many areas. The attitudes which the student takes towards his problems and withdrawal from or indifference towards the environment were closely related to adjustment.

Several investigators are of the opinion that academic adjustment or adjustment to college is an important factor in academic achievement. Students in general and under-achievers in particular have frequently reported problems of adjustment in college. Carson (1927) observed that on entering the college the freshman faces a number of new adjustment problems for which he is usually unprepared. Hence, Stogdill (1929), Angell (1930) and Philips (1930) emphasized the responsibility of the college to help in solving student's problems. Nagpal (1979) stated that the academic adjustment of undergraduate engineering students was an important correlate of over- and under-achievement.

Abraham (1974) revealed that the achievement level was associated with personal adjustment and social adjustment. Goswami (1978) reports that global self-concept and scholastic achievement had a significant positive correlation.

Reddy (1974) found academic adjustment significantly related to the scholastic performance of secondary school pupils. Soman (1977) also observed that personal adjustment variables had a considerable influence on achievement. Vashishtha (1991) found a positive relationship between adjustment and achievement.

In Salunke's (1979) study it was observed that educational facilities and emotional happiness in the home contributed positively to the academic achievement. Saun (1980) observed a significant difference between the high and the low achieving females in health, social, emotional and educational areas of adjustment.

Steinzer (1944), Cattell (1945) and Thompson (1948) pointed out that over-achievers were characterized by good adjustment to school and greater awareness and responsiveness to environmental influence. Frankel (1960) found that over-achievers conforming to school regulations adjusted better to the academic situation. Christenson (1956), Popham and Moore (1960) and Roberts (1962) observed that over-achievers differed, significantly from under-achievers in their adjustment to college. French (1958) considers that lack of adjustment to college life in the freshman introduces extraneous influences on scholastic success.

Berger and Sutker (1956) observed that students with adequate personality adjustment achieved better in academic performance. Brown (1953), Wellington (1965) and Graff (1957) demonstrated that high-achievers tend to be more stable and adjusted than low-achievers. Scott (1958) felt that only the best mode of adjustment maximizes the chance of success.

Soman's (1977) study revealed that the dominant personality factor identified for the over-achievers was individual adjustment factor. Dhami (1974) concluded that there was a higher relationship between scholastic achievement and emotional stability in the case of 9th class boys than in the case of 10th class boys who were more anxiety-ridden due to the coming public examinations. George (1966) mentioned that the pupils of 10th class with high intelligence were identified as better adjusted and higher achievers. Goswami (1978) found that scholastic achievement is highly correlated with the concept of adjustment.

Congdon (1943), Houston and Marzolf (1944), Hibler and Larson (1944) and Caroll and Jones (1944) have found several adjustment problems associated with under-achievement. Johnson (1947) held that poor performance in college was due to unsatisfactory adjustment in college. Anderson (1951) observed that many under-achievers were not beset with serious personal problems. Wig and Nagpal (1972) found that the failure group had poor adjustment at school and college but not at university.

Assum and Levy (1947) found personal adjustment positively related to scholastic achievement. Even when the typically maladjusted student was above his more fortunate fellow student, intellectually he often fell below the normal achievement. Stagmen (1953) found that unstable and maladjusted students had done less well than their stable contemporaries.

Martin (1952) held personal maladjustment bordering on neuroticism as characteristic feature of failing students. Jenson

(1958) reported a general tendency for non-achievers to encounter more adjustment problems.

Abraham (1974) observed that group adjustment, socio-personal adjustment were found to be the factors responsible for explaining total variance in the case of under-achievers.

Bhagirath (1979) found that the teachers and the students perceived the correlates of academic achievement as intelligence, character, creativity, punctuality, activeness, alertness, efficiency, educational adjustment, school and social adjustment, social/emotional adjustment and intelligence/social adjustment.

Majority of the above studies were tried to identify the relationship between achievement and adjustment either at school level or at college level, but they did not try to find out the association of these two variables in the samples of +2 students studying in residential and non-residential junior colleges.

ACHIEVEMENT AND INSTITUTIONAL CHARACTERISTICS

Researchers, of late, have been trying to identify what types of variables, interacting in the environment of an educational institute, affect the achievement of students and to what extent, which is to be most welcomed in the present day educational set-up and scientific environment.

Rani (1980) and Shasidhar (1981) concluded that the academic achievement was influenced by institutional factors with the sample of schedule caste students.

Reddy (1981) studied the interrelationship between organizational climate, socio-economic status, students' perception of rewarding behaviour and the academic achievement of a random stratified sample of 1607 pupils from 103 schools of Telangana area in A. P. and concluded that academic achievement level of schools having the organizational climate profile of (i) controlled, (ii) controlled-cum-paternal-cum-closed, (iii) controlled-cum-autonomous, and (iv) controlled-cum-open to be 305.34, 303.47, 325.73 and 364.54 respectively out of a total of 600 marks.

Desai (1979) and Hirunval (1980) observed a positive relationship between classroom climate and pupils' academic achievement in their studies conducted in Gujarat. Pal (1982) identified that good schooling, interest and industriousness played an important role in the learning of science. He also concluded that students belonging to the advanced schools had done better in science achievement test than those in less-advanced schools having the same or more or less identical general ability.

Subramanyam's (1981) study highlighted the importance of conditions at school vis-a-vis pupils' achievement. Multiple regression analysis of the data showed that personal characteristics of the children contributed to a large extent to their reading achievement and between the two factors, namely, school condition and home condition, and an increase in school condition was likely to lead to better achievement. In another study made by Srinivasa Rao and Subramanyam (1982) it was revealed that among the school factors, accommodation, educational level and experience of teachers, availability of instructional material, books and reading room facilities influenced the reading attainment of children positively.

Another study on classroom climate conducted in Rajasthan with a sample of 1294 by Verma (1977) concludes as : the rural school classes showed slight superiority over the urban school classes as far as acceptance, trustfulness, adaptability and emotional relationship dimensions of the classroom climate were concerned; the academic achievements of the urban and rural schools were at par but there was significant difference in the intellectual standards of the rural and the urban pupils; the mean differences of the classroom climate for adaptability and emotional relationship were significant in favour of the classrooms of the private schools; the classes of the privately managed schools had a more learning-conducive climate; the socio-emotional climate of the classroom not only predicted and influenced the pupil's academic achievement but also affected his classroom behavioural development; the classroom climate was positively correlated with the studiousness factor of the sociometric test; the classroom climate was negatively correlated with the behavioural development of the pupils in the class and also with the mischievousness factor; the pupils' classroom behaviour was positively correlated with their academic achievement. All the components of the studiousness factor and the composite studiousness factor were positively correlated and the mischievousness factor and its components were negatively correlated with the pupils' academic achievement.

All the studies discussed above highlight the importance of environment provided by the educational institution itself in the promotion of better achievement. But the question still remains as to which type of institutional climate affects the achievement, and to what extent, and so on. Further questions to be raised to the optimal achievement could be expected by the interaction effects of the student's background with different types of institutional or classroom climates.

RESEARCH DESIGN

Design is the heart of any research. For the present study the following aspects have been discussed which are concerned with the design of the study. Research procedures include the operational definitions of different terms used, the hypotheses that are framed for testing and the rationale of the formulated hypotheses. Selection of the samples includes the sampling techniques used, the reasons for selection of a particular sampling technique, and the selection of samples according to variables. Selection of tools includes the selection of suitable tools for collection of data, description of the tools selected, testing their suitability for the present study, and the procedure followed in administering the tools to collect the data required for the study.

The present study is divided into four areas to study them in depth in a specific and concrete way. The four areas are - socio economic status and achievement, educational aspirations and achievement, adjustment and achievement, and achievement of the students of residential and non - residential junior colleges.

Before going into the details of the samples, sampling techniques, variables, hypotheses and tools, it will be worthwhile if we discuss the operational definitions of the key terms used in the study which will enlighten the characteristics involved in each term.

OPERATIONAL DEFINITIONS

The operational definitions of the important terms used in the study are defined and discussed herewith.

Achievement

Achievement in an educational institution may be taken to mean any desirable learning that is observed in the student. Since the word desirable implies a value judgement, it is obvious that a particular learning may be referred to as achievement or otherwise depending on whether it is considered desirable or not. Understood in this way, any behaviour that is learned may come within the scope of achievement. Achievement, according to Smith (1969), and Spencer and Helmrich (1983), is the task-oriented behaviour that allows the individual's performance to be evaluated according to some internally or externally imposed criterion, that involves the individual in competing with others, or that otherwise involves some standard of excellence (Morgan, et al., 1986).

There is no gainsaying the fact that learning is not limited to mere acquisition of information, it also includes attitudes, interests, values, etc. Modern personality characteristics of the individual are learned. Therefore, the acquisition of desirable characteristics is as much an achievement as is knowledge of the principles of science or facts, world history or language and literature. Although achievement is used in this broad sense it is customary for schools and colleges to be concerned to a great extent with the development of knowledge, understanding and acquisition of skills (Narayana Rao, 1980). This may be in part owing to the fact that in the intellectual field the teacher can be relatively more certain of achieving the objectives he had set for himself than in other areas or domains.

The teacher or the institution has certain objectives which are often stated as the development of desirable characteristics of personality. Though this is undoubtedly a worthy goal, it is doubtful whether anything beyond the most superficial change could be obtained with the small number of hours contact between the teacher and the taught in the college. Thus in practice, the objectives are necessarily restricted to the imparting of various types of subject-matter knowledge.

Academic achievement is related to the acquisition of principles and generalizations and the capacity to perform efficiently, certain manipulations of objects, symbols and ideas. Assessment of academic performance has been largely conformed to the evaluation in terms of information, knowledge and understanding. It is universally accepted that the acquisition of factual data is not an end in itself but an individual who has received education should show evidence of having understood them. But, for obvious reasons, the examinations are largely confined to the measurement of the amount of information which students have acquired.

Wood and Learned (1938) concluded from their well known Pennsylvania study that education was unavoidably intellectual in which knowledge was the dominating feature of educational outcomes. It is perhaps the only accepted basis of promotion or fulfillment of requirements for degree or diploma. It is the actual or assumed possession of knowledge that counts for admission into a class or course. Educational measurements may be made with reference to either the aims or the results of education or both. The acquisition of knowledge consists of the registering of data or the making of a datum either more definite and indelible or meaningful. This conception of acquiring knowledge assumes that the student is an active organism in a stimulus-response situation, that the student interprets his experience, that he shows evidence of having registered and interpreted the datum by his appropriate response to it and that in future situations he will be guided by prior experience. Understood in this way measurement can be in terms of subject matter and this does not claim to minimize the importance of the other aspects of education.

Examinations in one form or another were employed by people ever since the days of early civilizations. Paul F. Cressey, a sociologist, attributes the remarkable stability of the old Chinese civilization among other things to her highly organized examination system. Examinations are not only used extensively, they vitally affect and determine the careers of students. From the earliest times teachers have examined as well as taught. Some kind of measurement or evaluation seems suitable in education and it is an essential part of the teaching, learning process.

Achievement in terms of subject matter is conventionally assessed in our institutions by employing a system of marks or grades. It has been strongly argued that marks are necessary for effective teaching, learning. Trabue (1926) felt that, for classification, guidance and evidence of effort, marks are necessary. A Committee of Principals of California listed the purposes of marks as the indication of the degree of mastery of subject matter and the prediction of future success. Madsen (1930) points out that marks set goals and motivate the students. Symonds (1927) listed among the purposes of marks, incitement of study, promotion of competition, determination of promotion, assistance in education and vocational guidance, awarding credits and honours. It is universally accepted that marks serve as the basis of classification and certification, motivation and measurement of educational performance.

Socio-Economic Status

Society is an organization of interacting people whose activities centre around a set of common goals and who tend to share common beliefs, attitudes and modes of action (Kuppuswamy, 1980). It is obvious that the society limits the activities of the individuals, by setting up standards which they have to follow and maintain. Thus society is a system of usages and procedures and involves authority as well as mutual aid. There are many groups of people, doing different kinds of work and following different kinds of norms in a complex and pluralistic society. In many societies, stratification is a characteristic feature. The phenomena involved in social stratification are chiefly, patterned interaction and stratum consciousness. Each stratum has free interactions with the members of that stratum and restrained interactions with members belonging to the strata superior to it as well as with those inferior to it. This is because there are different styles of life in the different strata of society with respect to education, occupation, possession, recreations and manners.

These characteristics are there in the social life whether it is organized on the basis of either caste or class. These differences are based on upbringing, education, occupation and income. While in the Indian caste system the strata are 'closed' groups, in the modern class system the strata are 'open' groups with opportunities for social mobility.

Another significant characteristic of the so-called casteless and classless societies, like the American or Soviet societies, is that the large majority consists of what the Americans call the middle class and what the Soviets call the working class.

The concept of stratification is closely linked with the concept of status. In a broad way it may be asserted that social status accrues to a person on the basis or the possession by him, of the characteristics valued by his society. Thus, the term status is meaningful in every kind of society. Status may be based on strength and skill or on the basis of the possession of land and wealth or on the basis of education and knowledge and so on. Every society, whether rural or urban, whether industrial or agricultural, has a status system. People are recognized as differing in status, some being perceived as of superior status and some as of inferior status.

The objective characteristics most frequently used are education, occupation and income. This is why it is called socio - economic status.

Educational Aspirations

Left to their own devices, most children would live in the present and let the future take care of itself. But they are not left to their own devices. Even before they enter school, parents, relatives and family friends ask children what they are planning to do when they are grown up. Most adults regard a child who says, " I want to be the Prime Minister or President" or "I am going to be a doctor or an engineer", as ambitious, and as courageous.

In a culture which provides vast opportunities for its members to be and to achieve what they want, it is understandable that children at an early age are subjected to pressures to create aspirations for the future. Aspirations, it is believed, motivate children to take advantage of the opportunities which the parents and the society provide.

Social pressures to plan for the future are reinforced by competition with members of the peer group in play and school or college-work. As the students compare what they can do with what their peers can do, it adds new meanings to their aspirations and puts new emphasis on the creation of aspirations that are both ego satisfying and admired by members of the social group. Thus, forming aspirations becomes an important area of creativity in students.

To the layman, aspiration is synonymous with ambition. It suggests that the person is not only planning personal betterment but also is carrying out this plan in real life. In the strictest sense, as used by the psychologists, ambition means a desire for honour, power or attainment. By contrast, aspiration means longing for what is above one, with advancement as its goal (Hurlock, 1978). Aspiration emphasizes the desire to improve or to rise above one's present status.

If aspiration and ambition were synonymous, and meant honourable attainment, people would be satisfied if their achievements were recognized and applauded by others. Children, for example, would be satisfied if their parents or relatives praised them for the houses they built in sand or with blocks, or for the drawings they made. If , on the other hand, the desire to improve or to have what is above one is taken into consideration, children would not necessarily be satisfied with their houses or drawings just because their parents praised them. Instead, they would be satisfied only if their houses or drawings met with the standards they set for themselves. This distinction is important because it helps to explain much of the dissatisfaction children - as well as adolescents and adults - experience in connection with their achievements and why, as a result, aspirations play such a large role in personal and social adjustments.

Aspirations are influenced by personal factors like - wishes for what individuals want to achieve; personal interests, which influence the areas of aspirations; past experiences with successes strengthening aspirations and failures weakening them; the personality pattern, which influences both the kind and the strength of aspirations; personal values, which determine what aspirations are important; sex, with boys aspiring higher than girls; socio-economic status, with those of the middle and upper groups aspiring higher than those of the lower groups; and racial background, with those of minority group status often aspiring unrealistically high as a form of compensation.

Aspirations are also influenced by the environmental factors such as parental ambitions, which are higher for first-born than later-born children; social expectations which emphasize that those who are successful in one area can be successful in all areas if they wish; peer pressures to set aspirations in areas important to the peer group; group emphasis on sex appropriateness of aspirations; cultural traditions which hold that all people can achieve anything they wish if they try hard enough; social values, which vary with the area of achievement; mass media, which encourages achievement aspirations; social rewards for high achievement and social neglect or rejection for low achievement; competition which siblings and peers view in the hope of showing one's superiority over them.

Aspirations, say for achievement or so, are influenced more by environmental factors than by personal factors. Some environmental influences encourage the development of immediate aspirations and some encourage remote aspirations; foster positive aspirations while others foster negative aspirations; some motivate the individual to be realistic and others to be unrealistic. In early childhood, before children are old enough to know what their abilities, interests and values are, their aspirations are largely shaped by their environments. As children grow older and are more aware of their abilities and interests, personal factors have a greater influence, but many of their aspirations are still environmental in origin.

Aspirations vary not only in strength but, even more important, in kind. They may be positive or negative. In the former, the emphasis is on winning success or on doing better than one has done before, while in the latter, the emphasis is on avoiding failure. Immediate aspirations are goals which the person sets for the immediate future - today, tomorrow, next week, or next month - while remote aspirations are goals set for the future. Childhood aspirations are likely to be unrealistic because knowledge and experiences at this age are limited. Adulthood aspirations may be realistic or idealistic.

Aspirations may be of educational, vocational, professional, social, sexual, economic, etc. Educational aspirations include courses such as medicine and engineering, science and technology , civil services, social sciences to sculpture, tailoring to trade, clerk to corps, general officer to educational administrator, and so on.

Adjustment

The concept of adjustment is not a new one. It is one of those terms in psychology that has been a source of great confusion as the word has many meanings packed into it. Herbert Spencer introduced the term into scientific parlance in his 'Principles of Biology' in 1864. He defined that life is the continuous adjustment of the internal to the external relations. This lends itself to the suggestion that life is always modified to fit external circumstances and ignores the essence of civilization, which is the modification of the external world to suit internal needs and desires of man. It connotes, besides this, a mechanical relationship that may be linked to the adjustment of the volume of a radio or television. To conceive of adjustment in such mechanistic terms is not to understand the essence of human life. Also, there is an element of vagueness about it. William James therefore characterized the concept of adjustment as 'vagueness incarnate'. John Dewey pointed out that in growing cultures the effective people do not adjust to the environment but instead adjust the environment to suit their needs. Ruth Strang holds that adjustment is a process and not a state ...... adjustment is continuous throughout life. Living, thus is a process of adjustment. Symonds defined adjustment as a satisfactory relation of an organism to its environment. L. S. Shaffer opines that adjustment is the process by which living organism maintains a balance between its need and the circumstances that influence the satisfaction of these needs. Various concepts of adjustment depend upon the meaning that is read into the word satisfactory or on what constitutes a satisfactory relationship.

A satisfactory relationship may mean adaptation to the demands of reality. A biological view of adjustment would emphasize adaptation for need reduction. The efforts of the individual to adapt himself to the environment, to overcome frustration in achieving the gratification of his needs, may be called the adjustment process. The situation that offers a few frustrating barriers to the individual would be favourable and aids adjustment. The adjustment process is affected and modified by the individual's experiences and thus learning plays a significant part in aiding adjustment. The statistical concept of adjustment may be looked upon as conformity to the norm. An individual is well adjusted while the queer, eccentric, deviant, are poorly adjusted. From the cultural point of view adjustment is assessed when an individual is accepted by his cultural group, i.e., if he conforms to his group's conventions, modes, ideas, etc.

Adjustment involves effective adaptation. It consists in the reduction of inner needs, stresses and strains and in this sense, adjustment would be a unique pattern depending upon the personality and needs of the individual. As each individual differs, so his needs differ and consequently his adjustment differs. Understood in this way, adjustment would be a harmonious relationship of an individual to his environment which affords him comfortable life devoid of strain, stress, conflict and frustration.

An adjusted individual knows his own strength and limitations, respects himself and others, aspires reasonably, satisfies his basic needs, does not find faults with others, shows flexibility in behaviour, is capable of struggling against odd circumstances, possesses a realistic perception of the world, feels lovely with his surroundings, etc. The major areas of adjustment are --

Emotional adjustment - Emotions play a leading role in one's adjustment to self and his environment. An individual is said to be emotionally adjusted if he is able to express his emotions in a proper way at a proper time. It requires one's balanced emotional development and proper training in the outlet of emotions.

Health adjustment - One should be adjusted with health and physical aspects soundly. If an individual's physical development and abilities are in conformity with those of his peers, he does not feel any difficulty in his progress due to some defects or incapabilities in his physical organs but he enjoys the full opportunity of being adjusted.

Home adjustment - We all know that home is a source of greatest satisfaction and security to its members. The relationships among the family members and their ways of behaviour play a leading role in adjustment of an individual. All problematic and delinquent behaviour is the result of the adjustment, and maladjustment, to a great extent is the product of faulty rearing and uncongenial atmosphere at home.

Social adjustment - An individual's social adjustment can be ascertained by his social development and adaptability to the social environment. Social adjustment requires the development of social qualities and virtues in an individual. It also requires that one should be social enough to live in harmony with one's social beings and feel responsibility and obligation towards one's fellow people, society and country.

Socio-Economic Status Scale

The social status accrues to a man on the basis or the possession by him, of the characteristics valued by his society. The status may be based on strength and skill or on the basis of the possession of land and wealth or on the basis of education and knowledge and so on (Kuppuswamy, 1980). Every society, whether rural or urban, whether industrial or agricultural, has a status system. People are recognized as differing in status, some being perceived as of superior status and some as of inferior status.

Measurement of socio-economic status is a major operation in almost all researches related to social concept. According to Linton the whole concept of status has emerged in terms of social differentiation (Beena Shah, 1986). Socio-economic status scale preparators have incorporated variables like family size, education, occupation, social position, caste, land ownership, social participation and possessions. But to identify the correct categories and minimize the perceptual content in socio-economic status for its accurate measurement, limited variables like caste, occupation, education, income, possession and social participation are being used in socio-economic status scales.

Based on the information of the socio-economic status scale, the socio-economic status can be classified into five categories, viz., upper status, upper middle status, middle status, lower middle status and lower status.

The socio-economic status scale selected for this study was intended to identify the socio-economic status of the students of junior colleges.

Educational Aspirations Scale

It is human nature to aspire for something after something. Without having proper aspirations one cannot rise high in any field and earn prestige and fulfil his needs.

The aspirations range from social, cultural to technological and educational. The educational aspirations include becoming doctors, engineers, lawyers, professors, collectors, police officials, technicians, scientists, administrators, etc. The higher the aspirations, the greater is the ability of the students.

The educational aspirations scale selected for this study was meant for the study of the educational aspirations of the students studying in junior colleges.

Adjustment Inventory

Life presents a continuous chain of struggle for existence and survival says Charles Robert Darwin, the great biologist. This observation is very correct as we find in our day to day life. Every one of us strives hard for the satisfaction of his needs. In struggling to achieve something, if one finds that results are not satisfactory, one changes either one's goal or the procedure. By resorting to such means one protects one's self from the possible injury to one's ego, failure or frustration. It is a sort of shifting to more defensive position in order to face challenge of circumstances after getting failure in either attempt or attempts. This special feature of the living organism is referred to as adjustment.

The adjustment is a continual process by which a person varies his behaviour to produce a more harmonious relationship between his environment and himself. It is also a process by which a person maintains a balance between its need and the circumstances that influence the satisfaction of these needs. A balanced personality of a person is the result of proper adjustment of an individual to his environment.

Adjustment measurement is an important aspect in the field of education in order to guide the students in a desirable way. For this purpose adjustment scales or inventories are used which usually include home adjustment, health adjustment, social adjustment, emotional adjustment, occupational adjustment, school or college adjustment, etc. These adjustment inventories measure all or some of the above aspects of adjustment depending on the need or necessity of the study under study.

As the adjustment inventory was meant for the assessment of the adjustment of individuals, the adjustment inventory, viz,

Indian Adaptation of Bell's Adjustment Inventory, selected for this study, is meant for the assessment of the adjustment of the students of the junior colleges.

Achievement Test

The term achievement is often understood in terms of a student's scores in a certain test. If, for instance, a student is tested in two school subjects, say English and Mathematics and in one subject he gets 50% marks while in other 70% marks, it is understood that his achievement in English in which he gets 50% marks is not better than that in Mathematics in which he gets 70% marks. This is a loose way of understanding the concept of achievement. More intelligently understood, achievement means one's learning attainments, accomplishments, proficiencies, etc. Achievement is directly related to a pupil's growth and development in educational situations where learning and teaching are intended to go on simultaneously. Achievement involves aptitude for learning, readiness for learning and opportunity for learning (Bhatia, 1991). Besides these factors, it also involves health and physical fitness, motivation, special aptitude, and emotional balance.

Freeman (1965) defines a test of educational achievement as a test designed to measure knowledge, understanding, skills in a specified subject or group of subjects. Thus according to him, an educational achievement test measures an individual's knowledge and understanding or skills in a particular branch of knowledge. Further, Freeman is of the view that through educational achievement test, it is possible to ascertain how much does a person know after receiving education or training in a particular branch of knowledge. Standardized achievement tests are used to determine the degree of achievement in a specific subject matter (Smith, Krouse and Atkinson, 1969). Achievement tests (Best , 1982) attempt to measure what an individual has learned - his or her present level of performance.

Anastasi (1968) has discussed the various uses of achievement tests - achievement tests are used to ascertain the attainment of minimum performance standards. In other words, an achievement test is to find out whether an individual has attained the required ability in a given field of knowledge or activity. Another important use of an achievement test is to be seen when there is a need for selecting candidates in regard to certain jobs or courses.

An achievement test is also used for purposes of guidance and counselling. It has been found useful in remedial teaching programmes as well as in determining the class to which a student should be admitted into. Administration of these tests at regular intervals is helpful to the teachers in knowing the kinds of difficulties faced by the students in learning. Finally it may be stated that the achievement test may be used as an aid in the evaluation of teaching, the importance of instructional techniques, and the revision of curriculum content.

Residential Junior Colleges

In the residential junior colleges, students stay on in the college campus with their teachers instead of coming daily from their houses. So they spend all their time either on the college premises or in the hostels, and pursue studies under the constant supervision of teachers. Such colleges of Intermediate or +2 level are considered residential junior colleges.

Non-residential Junior Colleges

The students of these colleges are in the college campus only during instructional hours and spend their remaining time at home or at other places. Such colleges are considered non-residential junior colleges.

Private Junior Colleges

The junior colleges managed by private organizations or persons, either partially or totally, were included in private junior colleges. The government recognized junior colleges and government aided junior colleges, but managed by private persons, were also included under private junior colleges.

Government Junior Colleges

The junior colleges under the sole management of government officials were included in this category. So the colleges managed by the Government of Andhra Pradesh and the

Andhra Pradesh Residential Junior Colleges' Society established by the Government of Andhra Pradesh were included in this category.

VARIABLES OF THE STUDY

Variables are a necessary requisite for any worthwhile research for the purpose of comparison. For the present study the following variables are considered. They are: residential versus non-residential, private versus government, and boys' versus girls'. The rationale for choosing the above stated variables is discussed herewith.

Residential versus Non-Residential Junior Colleges

The residential junior colleges are supposed to be in better position in all aspects when compared with non-residential junior colleges. The students of the residential junior colleges stay in the college itself without going home after the regular classroom teaching learning activities. They stay with their lecturers all the time, except for a few hours, and study and clear off their doubts immediately either in the classroom or during study hours Contrary to this, the students of non-residential junior colleges stay outside the college except 5 or 6 hours, and spend their remaining time at their own will and interest. The students interested in studies usually get some doubts during their study at home, but they have to wait for quite a long time to clear them off. The delay in getting them cleared off sometimes leads to frustration or carelessness. This teaching learning aspect will definitely play an important role in the achivement of students.

The infra-structure, the laboratory and library facilities will also be better in residential junior colleges. In Andhra Pradesh, the government residential junior colleges were started offering the best education to the meritorious students by providing facilities conducive to the progress of each and every student. The same way was followed by the private managements which established a large number of private residential junior colleges excelling in results and in catching state ranks. The intelligent students will always be in a better position, as they are not mixed up with the lesser intelligent students, which is a general practice in non-residential colleges.

Considering the above facts, the students of residential and non-residential junior colleges were taken into consideration to study the achievement and achievement correlates of the students.

Private versus Government Junior Colleges

The reputation of private junior colleges is generally far superior when compared with that of the government junior colleges. In private junior colleges the students are exposed to better conditions and better study atmosphere. The laboratories and libraries will be better. If better facilities are not provided in private colleges, the parents will question the authorities concerned as they pay higher fees for their children.

The quality of teaching is also supposed to be better in private junior colleges. The lecturers take more interest in teaching in private colleges as they are always or to some extent in the fear of either losing their jobs or immediately being questioned by the management about the quality of their teaching.

Since the standard of teaching is supposed to be different in private and government junior colleges, the achievement and achievement correlates of the students will be different and hence this variable is taken into consideration for this study.

Boys versus Girls

In olden days, boys were educated and the girls were restricted to their kitchens by their adult community. Times changed and the adults recognized the importance of women's education. In the words of our late Prime Minister Pandit Jawaharlal Nehru, 'if you educate a man you educate only one person, if you educate a woman you educate the entire family'. In due course, women's education gained importance and many parents are encouraging their daughters to pursue higher education. Women are also showing excellence in all fields and their presence is felt almost in all fields.

As the physiological conditions, exposure to society, education and other aspects of girls and boys vary differently, there may be a significant difference in the performance. The boys may be exposed to the society to a larger extent, but the girls spend most of their time in going through books or helping their parents at home. These factors will show their influence on their mental development and performance.

It is especially important to study the level of achievement and educational aspirations and mostly their adjustment because they just enter the adolescent stage, which is otherwise known as the period of stress and strain. At this stage, this sample finds that they find it extremely difficult to adjust themselves in the society because they are accepted neither as adults nor as children. It is also familiar that girls mature faster than boys at the early adolescent stage, both physically and mentally. The above factors will have their own impact on the achivement, adjustment and educational aspirations. So, a comparison between boys and girls will reveal the differences existing in adjustment, educational aspirations and achivement.

HYPOTHESES OF THE STUDY

Hypotheses are the tentative conclusions intended for verification. In the following pages the four major hypotheses and their rationale are discussed. Each one of the hypotheses has been studied in further detail by forming sub-hypotheses under each hypothesis.

HYPOTHESIS 1

Achievement of Intermediate students will be good.

Achievement is a paramount importance, particularly in the present socio-economic and cultural contexts , and great emphasis is placed on achievement right from the beginning of the formal education. It is a task-oriented behaviour that allows the individual's performance to be evaluated according to some internally or externally imposed criterion, that involves some standard of excellence.

Achievement is related to the acquisition of principles and generalizations and the capacity to perform efficiently, certain manipulations of objects, symbols and ideas. Assessment of achievement has been largely conformed to the evaluation in terms of knowledge and understanding. It is universally accepted that the acquisition of factual data is not an end in itself but that an individual who has received education should show the evidence of having understood them. But, for obvious reasons the examinations are largely confined to the measurement of the amount of information acquired by students.

Achievement in terms of subject matter is conventionally assessed in our institutions by employing a system of marks or grades, and it has been strongly argued that marks are necessary for effective teaching learning. Marks also set goals and motivate the students. It is universally accepted that marks serve as the basis of classification and certification, measurement and analysis of educational achievement.

The students studying in residential junior colleges stay round the clock in college campus and they will be under a strict vigilance of the wardens and lecturers. The students go through the lessons regularly and get their doubts clarified. The resident lecturers also check the student's performance regularly. And at the same time these colleges will have well-equipped laboratories, libraries and other centres of learning.

Contrary to this, the students studying in non-residential colleges will be in the college for about 5 or 6 hours a day and the balance of the time will be spent according to their interest. As there will be no watch on their studies, these students do not try to study regularly and get their doubts clarified on the spot.

As stated earlier, under this area, the variables, namely, residential versus non-residential junior college students, private versus government junior college students and boys versus girls were considered. To study each of these variables in detail three sub-hypotheses were formulated for each hypothesis. They were stated in 'Null hypothesis' form. 'A Null hypothesis states that there is no significant difference or relationship between two or more parameters. It concerns a judgement as to whether apparent differences or relationships are true differences or relationships or whether they merely result from sampling error' (Best).

The following were the sub-hypotheses formulated in this area.

Hypothesis 1A

There is no significant difference in the level of achievement of the students of residential and non-residential junior colleges.

Hypothesis 1B

There is no significant difference in the achievement of the students of private and government junior colleges.

Hypothesis 1C

There is no significant difference in the achievement of boys and girls of junior colleges.

HYPOTHESIS 2

There will be a significant positive association between achievement and socio-economic status of junior college students.

The central characteristic of a society is that an organization of interacting people whose activities centre around a set of common goals and who tend to share common beliefs, attitudes and modes of action. It is stratified with different categories of status. Social status is accrued to a person on the basis of possession by him, land and wealth, strength and skill, education and knowledge, and so on. The objective characteristics mostly used are education, occupation and income.

A set of potentially influential factors for student's achievement are generally categorized as being associated either with home or college environment. It should, however, be noted that the distinction is more of convenience than of explanatory value. For one, the characteristics of the college that one attends tend to vary according to one's home background. For another, it is not themselves' but in relation to his experiences at college that many of the distinctive characteristics of a student's home environment may influence his academic performance.

Since the society in India consists of different classes, it is but natural for the researchers to think of the extent to which home conditions influence the academic achievement of the students. Sudame (1973) and Reddy (1974) found no significant correlations between socio-economic status and academic achievements. But, Satyanandan (1969), Menon (1973), Anand (1973), Abraham (1974), Basavayya (1974), Dave and Dave (1971), Chandra (1975), Chatterji, *et al.* (1971), Salunke (1979), Khanna (1980), Gupta (1982) and many other studies established a positive relationship between performance and socio-economic status of the family.

In an early study Sherman and Key (1932) tested children from several hollows in the Blue Ridge Mountains approximately one hundred miles from Washington, D.C. Life in this cultural setting was characterized by an extreme degree of poverty, low literacy, poor educational facilities, and isolation from other communities. Not surprisingly, then, the children achieved less than average scores, and performance was related to the cultural level of the individual hollows.

With this it seems clearly that there is a relationship between achievement and socio-economic status. But, here, the researchers wish to see this relationship in residential and non-residential junior college students, where this type of study did not take place.

Hypothesis 2A

There is no significant difference in the level of association between achievement and socio-economic status of the students of residential and non-residential junior colleges.

Hypothesis 2B

There is no significant difference in the level of association between achievement and socio-economic status of the students of private and government junior colleges.

Hypothesis 2C

There is no significant difference in the level of association between achievement and socio-economic status of boys and girls of junior colleges.

HYPOTHESIS 3

There will be a significant positive association between achievement and educational aspirations of junior college students.

Aspiration is a longing for what is above one, with advancement as its goal. It emphasizes the desire to improve or to rise above one's present status. It is a measure of one's intentional disposition, an important element of long range behaviour. It is necessary to have knowledge of the aspirational level of an individual, both from educational and from guidance point of view.

Unemployment, under-employment and unsuitable employment are some of the major problems of the educated youth. Educational institutions are charged with the responsibility of developing vocational behaviours which may solve some of these problems. Right type of educational and vocational choices therefore have come to occupy a central place in the life of students. Educational aspirations keep the student on the track of hard work to achieve the set goal. Depending on the social status, interests, capabilities, facilities, etc., the educational aspirations vary in a wide range from individual to individual.

Under this area, educational aspirations and achievement of junior college students, the following sub-hypotheses were framed.

Hypothesis 3A

There is no significant difference in the level of association between achievement and educational aspirations of the students of residential and non-residential junior colleges.

Hypothesis 3B

There is no significant difference in the level of association between achievement and educational aspirations of the students of residential and non-residential junior colleges.

Hypothesis 3C

There is no significant difference in the level of association between achievement and educational aspirations of boys and girls of junior colleges.

HYPOTHESIS 4

There will be a significant positive association between achievement and adjustment of junior college students.

The concept of adjustment is as old as the human race on the earth. Every human being seeks adjustment to various situations. He constantly makes efforts to adjust himself to his surroundings because a wholesome adjustment is essential for leading a happy life and gaining satisfaction. Satisfactory adjustment is characterized by a behaviour which is both adaptive and constructive. Adjustment is the outcome of the individual's attempts to deal with stress and meet his needs: also, his efforts to maintain harmonious relationship with the environment (Coleman, 1969). A good adjustment is one which is both realistic and satisfying. At-least in the long run, it reduces to a minimum the frustrations, tensions and anxieties which a person must endure. Adjustment develops in an individual through the influence of family, society, economics, school, religion, etc.

The school and the teacher have a great role in developing proper adjustment behaviour in a child. Moore reported in his study that nearly 80 per cent children of an infant school providing education to 6 to 11 years old had some difficulties in adjustment to the school situation (Rastogi, 1983). Mukherji found that adjustment is having correlation with achievement. A well adjusted individual excels in performance also.

Under this area the following sub-hypotheses were formulated.

Hypothesis 4A

There is no significant difference in the level of association between achievement and adjustment of the students of residential and non-residential junior colleges.

Hypothesis 4B

There is no significant difference in the level of association between achievement and adjustment of the students of private and government junior colleges.

Hypothesis 4C

There is no significant difference in the level of association between the achievement and adjustment of boys and girls of junior colleges.

SELECTION OF SAMPLE

After finalizing the variables of the present study, consideration was given to whether the entire population is to be made the subject for data collection or a particular group is to be selected as representative of the whole population. The 'entire population' here refers to all the Senior Intermediate students of Andhra Pradesh.

Selection of a group as a representative of the entire population was found to be more convenient and suitable. This technique leads to a considerable saving of time, effort and nance. The number of students selected is small, and so it is possible to make a detailed and intensive study. This generally leads to more accurate and reliable results. As this sampling technique has many advantages, it was selected for the collection of data.

In any social research, various methods are utilized for selection and drawing of samples. After a detailed study of all these methods, and considering the variables selected for the research work, the stratified sampling method was found most suitable. In the stratified sampling method, the entire population is divided into smaller homogeneous groups (Best) or strata, and then the sample is selected within each group. Every sampling unit in the population is placed in one of the strata prior to the selection of the sample so that the sum of the strata is identical with the population. Stratified sampling method has certain merits and advantages as a technique of sampling. Auckoff has rightly said that 'stratified sampling enables the researcher to make a comparison of properties of the strata as well as to estimate population characteristics (Kerlinger , 1964).

The investigators, in the stratified sampling method, have greater control over the selection of the sample when compared with random sampling. In random sampling, although every group has a chance of being selected and included in the sample, there is every possibility, and sometimes it does happen, that certain important groups are left unrepresented. But in stratified sampling method no important group is likely to be left out.

Stratified sampling method is the ideal one when comparison between different variables has to be made. For example, if comparison has to be made between residential and non-residential junior college students, it would be very difficult to select the required number of units through any other method of sampling. If any other method is used, the problem of bias and prejudice creeps in.

Replacement of units is also possible in the stratified sampling method. Normally if a particular unit is not accessible to a study, it is difficult to replace it by another, but in this method it is possible. Stephen states that 'stratification automatically brings about a replacement of persons lost to the sample, by persons of the same stratum, thus partly correcting the bias that would result if there were no replacements of losses (Festinger and Daniel, 1976). As the entire population is divided into particular strata it is easy and convenient to replace an inaccessible case by an accessible one.

In this stratified sampling method, much depends on the stratification process. The following precautions were taken while stratifying the population: the variables involved in the study were taken note of; care was taken to see that each stratum in the universe was large enough in size so that selection of items could be made on random basis; the strata formed were definite and clear cut; each stratum was free from the influence of the other; that there was no overlapping.

Before actually selecting the sample, certain fundamental principles were considered to make the sample scientific and clear-cut.

Firstly, the 'universe' is to be clearly defined. In the technical phraseology of research, the whole population out of which the samples are selected is known as the 'universe'. For the present research work, the universe includes all the students of senior Intermediate studying in residential and non-residential junior colleges of Andhra Pradesh. But, the study was limited to a particular geographical area to facilitate appropriate sample selection and to avoid bias and prejudice.

Secondly, a decision has to be made about the units of the sample. A unit of sample may be a house, a family, a group of individuals or a single individual. A good unit should possess the following characteristics ------ (A) Clarity: The unit should be clearly defined in unambiguous terms. This would make the study easy and efficient. For the present research work, a sampling unit was defined as a pupil of senior Intermediate studying in any college in Andhra Pradesh; (B) Suitability: A good unit should be well suited to the problem under study. Since the problem is related to the achievement of residential and non-residential senior Intermediate students, the unit selected is well suited to the problem; (C) Accessibility: The unit selected should be easily accessible to the researchers. If the units selected are difficult to reach and if the researchers fail to make use of them, the study would be vitiated. The selected sampling unit, i.e., a senior Intermediate student is easily accessible since the researchers could be approached in any junior college.

Thirdly , it is looked upon the availability or preparation of the source list. This is an important factor that makes the representative selection possible. A source list is the list which contains the names of the units of the universe from which the sample may be selected. It may exist even before the beginning of the project or it may be prepared afresh by the investigators. Without a source list, study through the sampling method is not possible. For the present research work, a source list, consisting of the names of residential junior colleges and non-residential junior colleges of Andhra Pradesh, was used. Care was taken to see that the source list was up-to-date and valid and that there was no repetition of the names of colleges. This source list was found to be relevant and suitable because it includes the colleges as the study deals with the senior Intermediate students.

Besides considering these principles, it is extremely important to think about the size of the sample to be selected. If the sample is either very small or very large, it will make the study difficult and will also make the results untenable. According to Parten 'an optimum sample in survey is the one which fulfils the requirements of effective representativeness, reliability and flexibility. The sample should be small enough to avoid intolerable sampling error'. The size of the sample for the present research work was decided after considering the following factors.

Since an intensive study was planned, a very large number of samples were not selected. In case of an intensive study, very large number of samples were not so useful as they involve huge consumption of the resources. A smaller sample was found to be convenient.

The size and selection of the samples are also influenced by the nature of the universe. If the universe is homogeneous, even a small-sized sample may yield dependable and required results. If the universe is heterogenous, small-sized samples may not be useful. In case of the present study, the homogenous universe was split into smaller homogeneous groups and the samples were selected from these groups. For example, all the senior Intermediate students were broadly grouped under residential and non-residential students. A sample was selected from each of these two groups.

The investigators need to determine the number of the groups to be formed. In case the number of groups proposed is large, the size of the samples shall have to be large so that every group should be of proper size and suit the requirements of the study. In case the number of groups proposed is small, even small-sized samples can fulfil the requirement. In the case of the present study, the number of groups into which the universe was divided are - girls and boys, private and government junior colleges and residential and non-residential junior colleges. Since the number of groups is more, a reasonable large sample was selected from each of these groups.

Practical considerations and accuracy also play a vital role in determining the size of the sample. Every study is guided by certain practical considerations such as time, resources, accessibility of data, etc. Usually, it is believed that a large-sized sample is more representative and generally produces accurate results. This, of course, depends upon the technique of sampling used. If the technique is scientific, even small-sized samples can produce dependable and accurate results. While selecting the size of the sample for the present study, practical considerations like the availability of resources and time were taken into consideration. Care was taken to make the sample selection technique as scientific as possible.

The size of the sample is also governed by the size of the tools to be used. In case the tools are short, and the questions asked pertain to certain limited factors, a large sample can be selected. In case the tools are large and the questions complicated, the sample should be small in size so that, from administrative point of view, the investigators may not be put to unnecessary troubles. In the present study, the tools were quite elaborate and large, hence a very large sample was not selected.

The sampling method also determines the size of the sample. When random sampling method is used, the samples have to be large. On the other hand if samples are selected through stratified sampling method, the reliability can be achieved even with the help of the small-sized samples.

Taking into consideration all these factors which influence the size of the sample, it was decided that an ideal sample would consist of six hundred students. This sample is small enough to avoid unnecessary expenditure and large enough to avoid intolerable sampling errors.

After deciding about the sampling method and the size of the sample, the universe selected was divided into different strata. The variables chosen for the study were considered to divide the universe. The variables chosen were - (1) boys versus girls, (2) government versus private junior colleges, (3) residential versus non-residential junior colleges.

Taking the variable which compares residential and non-residential junior college students at first instance, the Universe was split into residential and non-residential junior colleges. An equal number of samples was taken from residential and non-residential colleges, i.e., 300 from residential junior colleges and 300 from non-residential junior colleges.

Taking the variable which compares government and private junior colleges, the Universe selected consisted of the senior Intermediate students studying in government and private junior colleges of Andhra Pradesh. An equal number of samples was taken from both government and private junior colleges, i.e., 300 students from government colleges and 300 from private colleges.

To select the sub-samples, the Random Sampling Method was considered. In this method all the units from all types of junior colleges, viz., private and government junior colleges, and private and government residential junior colleges, were given equal importance. The individuals were chosen in such a way as each has an equal chance of being selected, and that each choice is independent of any other choice. Random sampling may be done with the help of many methods. The lottery method suggested by Best was used in this study.

It was decided to select 24 colleges for the collection of sample. Out of these 24 colleges, 6 were private non-residential and 6 were government non-residential colleges, and 8 were private residential junior colleges and 4 were government residential junior colleges.

As there is only one co-educational government residential junior college, girls are to be selected from that college only. The remaining residential junior college girls are to be selected from private residential junior colleges. In this method the names of private residential junior colleges were written on slips of equal size, the slips were wound round, well mixed, and kept in a container. As per the schedule, 8 slips from the container were picked up to select eight private residential junior colleges. In the same manner other types of colleges were selected. From each college, it was decided to select 25 senior Intermediate students.

Following the above sampling procedure, 600 senior Intermediate students were selected as sample for this study. Out of these 600 senior Intermediate students, 300 were from residential junior colleges and 300 were from non-residential junior colleges. 300 boys were selected equally from residential and non-residential junior colleges. Girls were also selected from residential and non-residential colleges, but as there is only one government residential junior college which admits girls as co-educators equal number of girls were not selected equally from the government and private residential colleges. Twenty five girls were selected from the government residential junior college and 125 were selected from private residential junior colleges. The following table gives the details of the sample distribution.

Table 1 : Distribution of Sample

Total Senior Intermediate Students
600

Boys 300				Girls 300			
Residential 150		Non-Residential 150		Residential 150		Non-Residential 150	
Govt	Private	Govt	Private	Govt	Private	Govt	Private
75	75	75	75	25	125	75	75

The sampling design employed thus involved not only the stratification of the universe but also random sampling technique to select samples from within the stratum.

SELECTION OF TOOLS

Research tools are the sole factors in determining sound data and in drawing accurate conclusions about the problem in hand. The conclusions ultimately help in providing suitable remedial measures to the problem concerned.

The selection and use of tools can be done in two ways. The first one is to construct a tool independently by the researchers for their own study. Here, there are many problems in doing so. Preparation and standardization of a perfect tool itself is a major task, and one can say that it is a doctoral study itself. On construction of their own tools, Anand and Padma feel that 'a note of caution has to be struck when a researcher develops a tool for his study by merely pooling some items and does not subject it to the sophisticated techniques of tool construction. The result will be then obvious, a poor quality research'.

The second way of selection and use of tools is the right selection of tools from already standardised ones available in the field of study. Here also, it involves a tedious job in locating the tools and identifying their usefulness to the study on hand. Even then, this technique is very useful when a research work involves a good number of variables. Some people believe that some of the instruments available do not measure upto their standards. Hence, new ones. In some instances, consideration should be given to the logistics of the situation. Lacking in the time and financial resources of a test and measurement organisation or researcher, many researchers cannot expect to produce a better instrument. In these cases, the most logical procedure that can be followed is to choose the best instrument available for the purpose (Pearl, 1974).

Considering the flaws and the merits of the selection of tools, the investigators are interested in using the standardized tools as the present study involves an intensive study of socio-economic status, educational aspirations, adjustment and performance of the senior Intermediate students studying in residential and non-residential junior colleges.

Measurment of Socio-Economic Status

After a thorough survey of literature, the investigators identified the following tools on socio-economic status which were found to be useful primarily. They include Kuppuswamy, Verma, Kulshresta, Shrivastava, Singh and Saxena, Udai Pareek and Trivedi, Rao, Patel, and Beena Shah. Among the tools available on SES prepared in Indian context, the SES developed by Beena Shah was found most suitable for the present study as it contains all necessary aspects that contribute to the socio-economic status of an individual and as it was prepared more scientifically than any other tool considering the flaws of the SES scales.

The Socio-Economic Status scale thus selected was subjected to pretesting, which is, infact, a 'dress rehearsal' of the final study (Goode and Hatt, 1952). The SES was administered to a sample of one hundred senior intermediate students. The reliability of SES was found as 0.91 as calculated by test-retest method. As this result was very close to the test result, the Socio-Economic Status scale of Beena Shah (1986) was finalised for the final administration to measure the socio-economic status of the sample.

Measurement of Educational Aspirations

To measure the educational aspirations of the senior Intermediate students, an extensive survey was made to find out the suitable tool for this study. Through this survey, it was found that tools prepared on educational aspirations by Saxena, Sharma, Gupta and Srivastava and Vansal are available for use in research studies. Out of these tools, it was identified that the educational aspirations tool prepared by S.K. Saxena (1986) was suitable for this study.

Later, after identifying the suitability of the tool, the tool was administered to a sample of 100. The reliability of the tool in our conditions was found as 0.88. As this result is nearer to the tool result, it was finalised to use if in this study to measure the educational apirations of the senior Intermediate students.

Measurement of Adjustment

The review of the related research tools reveals that there are many tools in India on Adjustment. Out of them, initially, Adjustment inventories prepared by Srivastava and Govind Tiwari, Indian Adaptation of Bell's Adjustment Inventory (Lalita Sharma), Singh, Kumar, Jain, Pal, Patil, Pandey and Bhagia were selected and the contents were studied in detail. Through this study, Indian Adaptation of Bell's Adjustment Inventory of Lalita Sharma (1989) was found suitable for the study.

After finalysing the inventory, it was administered on a sample of 100 senior Intermediate students. The data was tested for reliability by using split-half method and the reliability was found as 0.89. As this result has a close relationship with the reliability of the test, this Adjustment Inventory was finalised to use in the present study.

Measurement of Achievement

To measure the achievement, marks of the Intermediate public examinations of the sample were taken. These marks were taken because these were achieved by the sample from the common public examination conducted by the Board of Intermediate Education, it being a testing organisation established by the Governement of Andhra Pradesh. And two more factors taken into consideration while taking these marks were : (1) The other tests viz., Socio-Economic Status scale, Educational Aspirations Scale and Adjustment Inventory involve a lot of time and labour on the part of the students as they were very long and critical, and (2) as the investigators intend to compare the performance of the residential and non-residential junior college students they need only the achievement of the students of residential and non-residential junior colleges which is based on a standard common public examination.

The tools viz., Socio Economic Status Scale of Beena Shah, Indian Adaption of Bell's Adjustment Inventory of Lalita Sharma, Education Aspirations Scale of S.K. Saxena and the marks of Intermediate Public Examination, were finalised for the collection of data.

DATA COLLECTION

The tools were administered on the sample personally, but the marks of the senior Intermediate public exams were collected later from the principals concerned.

DATA ANALYSIS

The organisation, analysis and interpretation of data and formulation of conclusions and generalizations are necessary steps to get a meaningful picture out of the raw information collected. The analysis and interpretation of data involve the objective material in the possession of the researcher and his subjective reactions and desires to derive from the data the inherent meanings in their relation to the problem (Rummel, 1958).

The mass data collected through the use of various tools, need to be systematized and organized, i.e., edited, classified and tabulated before it can serve the purpose. Here editing implies the checking of gathered data for accuracy, utility and completeness; classifying refers to the dividing of the information into recording of the classified material in accurate mathematical terms. Analysis of data means studying the tabulated material in order to determine inherent facts or meanings. It involves breaking down the existing complex factors into simpler parts and putting the parts together in new arrangements for purposes of interpretation.

After the data collection was finished, it was analysed keeping in view the objectives and hypotheses of the study. The present study includes four major aspects, viz., achievement, socio-economic status, educational aspirations and adjustment. From the tools used, the total scores of socio-economic status, educational aspirations and adjustment were taken as raw scores for each candidate. The total marks of senior Intermediate public examinations of each student were collected from the respective colleges.

These four types of raw scores were used as basic sources of data for the study of the said areas. These raw data were put to statistical treatment. The hypotheses framed were statistically tested and accordingly accepted or rejected. The data was thus statistically treated and the results were presented in the following pages.

ACHIEVEMENT

The total marks of senior Intermediate public examination of each student were taken to find out the achievement status of total sample as well as each sub-sample. The maximum score that a student can get is 1000 and the minimum is 1. In the present study the highest score secured by a student studying in Vignan Residential Junior College, Vadlamudi, Guntur District was 929. This was the A.P. State's First Rank in Intermediate Public Examination. The lowest mark secured by a student was 418.

For the purpose of classification of achievement into 3 categories, viz., low , average and high the following procedure was followed. As the sample was selected only from science and mathematics groups , the students scored very well. Hence the categorisation was made as - a student who scored 499 and below (third class) was put in low achievement group, who scored between 501 and 719 (second and first classes) was kept in average achievement group, and who scored 720 and above (distinction) was placed in high achievement group.

The mean scores were used to identify the achievement status of total sample and to compare the sub-sample variation. The values of standard deviation were used to measure the spread or dispersion of scores in the distribution (Best). The critical ratios were calculated to test the significant difference in the means of the two sub-samples of each variable.

The chi-square (X^2) test of independence was applied for comparing the experimentally obtained results with those to be expected theoretically on some hypothesis (Garret, 1979).

HYPOTHESIS 1: Achievement of Intermediate students will be good.

To test the validity of the Hypothesis 1, the total marks of all the samples were calculated to arrive at mean and standard deviation of the sample. The results are as follows.

Table 2: Achievement of the Whole Sample

Sample	Sample size	Mean	Standard Deviation
Whole	600	727.22	68.31

It is clear, from the above table, that the Intermediate Science and Mathematics students studying in junior colleges were high in achievement. But, as per standard deviation, the dispersion of scores was great in the units of the sample.

The chi-square test of independence was applied to test the divergence of observed results from those expected theoritically.

Table 3 : Distribution of Achievement in the Whole Sample

Sample Size		Low	Average	High	X^2
600	f_o	1	283	316	636.4*
	f_e	96	408	96	

*Significant at 0.01 level

f_o = frequency of occurence of observed or experimentally determined facts

f_e = frequency of occurence expected theoretically

As the chi-square test value was significant, the achievement of Intermediate students was not distributed normally. The achievement trend was tending towards high achievements.

The hypothesis that *the achievement of Intermediate students will be good* can be accepted.

HYPOTHESIS 1A: There is no significant difference in the level of achievement of the students of residential and non-residential colleges.

To compare the difference in the level of achievement in residential and non-residential college students, the following statistical treatment was given.

Table 4 : Comparison of Achievement of Residential and Non-Residential College Students

Variable	Sample size	Mean	Standard Deviation	Mean Difference	SED	Critical Ratio
Residential	300	751.75	61.74			
Non-Residential	300	702.69	65.80	49.06	5.2	9.43*

* Significant at 0.01 level

It is clear, from the above table, that there was a great significant difference in the level of achievement in the students studying in residential and non-residential colleges. The students of residential colleges were better in achievement than those of non-residential colleges.

As a great difference was seen in the level of achievement in the variables, the distribution of it was studied in both the sub-samples.

Table 5: Distribution of Achievement in Residential and Non-Residential College Students

Variable	Sample size		Low	Average	High	X^2
Residential	300	f_o	0	85	215	698.43*
		f_e	48	204	48	
Non-Residential	300	f_o	1	117	122	163.67*
		f_e	48	204	48	

* Significant at 0.01 level

The distribution of achievement was not normal in both the cases. The ahievement concentration in residential colleges was very high in high achievement group and it was almost equal in average and high achievement groups in non-residential colleges.

The hypothesis that *there is no significant difference in the level of achievement of the students of residential and non-residential junior colleges* can be rejected.

HYPOTHESIS 1B: There is no significant difference in the level of achievement of the students of private and government junior colleges.

A comparison was made to identify the difference in the level of achievement of the students studying in private and government colleges. The results are as follows.

Table 6 : Comparison of Achievement of Private and Government College Students

Variable	Sample size	Mean	Standard Deviation	Mean Difference	SED	Critical Ratio
Private	350	744.47	66.14			
				41.39	5.38	7.69*
Government	250	703.08	63.96			

*Significant at 0.01 level

As per the mean scores and value of critical ratio, there was a great difference in the level of achievement in the students of private and government colleges.

As there was difference in the level of achievement in the sub-samples, it was tried to identify the distribution of achievement in the students of private and government colleges.

Table 7: Distribution of Achievement in Private and Government College Students

Variable	Sample size		Low	Average	High	X^2
		f_o	0	133	217	
Private	350					1136.39*
		f_e	56	238	56	
		f_o	1	150	99	
Government	250					127.4*
		f_e	40	170	40	

*Significant at 0.01 level

Table - 7 states that the distribution of achievement in the sub-samples was not normally distributed as the chi-square values were very highly significant. In private colleges the achievement concentration was in the high achievement group, but in the government colleges it was in the average achievement group.

The hypothesis that *there is no significant difference in the level of achievement of the students of private and government junior colleges* can be rejected.

HYPOTHESIS 1C: There is no significant difference in the level of achievement of boys and girls of junior colleges

A comparison was made to identify the difference in the achievement of boys and girls. The data are as follows.

Table 8: Comparison of Achievement of Boys and Girls

Variable	Sample size	Mean	Standard Deviation	Mean Difference	SED	Critical Ratio
Boys	300	739.15	73.59			
				23.85	5.49	4.34*
Girls	300	715.30	60.40			

*Significant at 0.01 level

According to the mean scores and critical ratio there was a difference in the achievement of boys and girls.

As there was difference in the achievement of boys and girls, it was tried to identify the distribution of achievement in both the sub-samples.

Table 9 : Distribution of Achievement in Boys and Girls

Variable		Sample	Low	Average	High	X^2
		f_o	11	121	178	
Boys	300					414.3*
		f_e	48	204	48	
		f_o	0	162	138	
Girls	300					397.45*
		f_e	48	204	48	

* Significant at 0.01 level

As per the chi-square value, boys were slightly better in achievement. In boys the achievement concentration was in high achievement group, where as it was in average achievement groups in girls.

The hypothesis that *there is no significant difference in the level of achievement of boys and girls of junior colleges* can be rejected.

ACHIEVEMENT AND SOCIO-ECONOMIC STATUS

The present study aims at identifying the association between achievement and socio-economic status. The chi-square test of independence was applied to identify the association between these two areas. The chi-square values and results are given below.

HYPOTHESIS 2: **There will be a significant positive association between achievement and socio-economic status of junior college students.**

To test the validity of this hypothesis the chi-square value was computed for the whole sample.

Table 10: Association between Achievement and SES in the Whole Sample

Sample	Sample size	X^2
Whole	600	61.854*

* Significant at 0.01 level

The chi-square value mentioned in the above table indicates that there was a positive and high association between the socio-economic status and achievement of the students studying in junior colleges.

The hypothesis that *there will be a significant positive association between socio-economic status and achievement* can be accepted.

HYPOTHESIS 2A: There is no significant difference in the level of association between achievement and socio-economic status of the students of residential and non-residential junior colleges.

To test the validity of Hypothesis 2A the chi-square values were computed and are given here under.

Table 11: Association between Achievement and SES in Residential and Non-residential College Students

Variable	Sample size	X^2
Residential	300	29.151*
Non-Residential	300	38.424*

*Significant at 0.01 level

It is clear from the chi-square values that there was a significant positive association between achievement and socio-economic status.

The association between achievement and socio-economic status in non-residential junior colleges was a little bit more when compared with its counter part, residential junior colleges.

The hypothesis that ***there is no significant difference in the level of association between achievement and socio-economic status of the students of residential and non-residential junior colleges*** **can be rejected.**

HYPOTHESIS 2B: There is no significant difference in the level of association between achievement and socio-economic status of the students of private and government junior colleges.

The chi-square values were calculated to test the validity of Hypothesis 2B, which are given below.

Table 12: Association between Achievement and SES in Private and Government College Students

Variable	Simple Size	X^2
Private	350	27. 161*
Government	250	24.634*

* Significant at 0.01 level

From the above table it seems that there was a significant positive association between achievement and socio-economic status of the students studying in private and government colleges.

It also seems from the above table that the difference in the association of achievement with socio-economic status in the private college students and government college students was very negligible. The small amount of difference in the association between achievement and socio- economic status may be due to the difference in sample size.

The hypothesis that *there is no significant difference in the level of association between achievement and socio-economic status of the students of private and government junior colleges* can be accepted.

HYPOTHESIS 2 C: **There is no significant difference in the level of association between achievement and socio - economic status of boys and girls of junior colleges.**

To test the validity of the Hypothesis 2C, chi-square values were computed and are given herewith.

Table 13: Association between Achievement and SES in Boys and Girls

Variable	Sample size	X^2
Boys	300	50.37*
Girls	300	16.04*

* Significant at 0.01 level

The association between achievement and socio-economic status was quite evident in both boys and girls.

When compared the association between achievement and socio-economic status of boys with girls, the association was very high in boys.

The hypothesis that ***there is no significant difference in the level of association of achievement and socio-economic status of boys and girls of junior colleges*** **can be rejected.**

ACHIEVEMENT AND EDUCATIONAL ASPIRATIONS

The present study was also intended to identify whether there exists any association between achievement and educational aspirations. For this the values of chi-square test of independence were computed, by which the association between these two areas was to be identified. The statistical data and their results are given below.

HYPOTHESIS 3: **There will be a significant positive association between achievement and educational aspirations of junior college students**

The chi-square value was computed for the whole sample to test the validity of the above hypothesis.

Table 14: Association between Achievement and Educational Aspirations in the Whole Sample

Sample	Sample size	X^2
Whole	600	89.354*

* Significant at 0.01 level

The chi-square value available from the table indicates that there was a significant relationship between achievement and educational aspirations of the students studying in junior colleges.

The hypothesis that ***there will be a significant positive association between achievement and educational aspirations*** **can be accepted.**

HYPOTHESIS 3A: **There is no significant difference in the level of association between achievement and educational aspirations of the students of residential and non-residential colleges.**

To test the validity of the Hypothesis 3A, the chi-square value was calculated and it is given herewith.

Table 15: Association between Achievement and Educational Aspirations of Residential and Non-residential College Students

Variable	Sample size	X^2
Residential	300	25.305*
Non-Residential	300	51.723*

* Significant at 0.01 level

The association between achievement and educational aspirations was significant in the students studying in both residential and non-residential junior colleges.

The difference in the association between achievement and educational aspirations of the students studying in residential colleges was lesser than those studying in non-residential colleges.

The hypothesis that *there is no significant difference in the level of association between achievement and educational aspirations of the students of residential and non-residential junior colleges* can be rejected.

HYPOTHESIS 3B: **There is no significant difference in the level of association between achievement and educational aspirations of the students of private and government junior colleges.**

Chi-square values were calculated to test the validity of the Hypothesis 3B and the chi-square values are given here under.

Table 16: Association between Achievement and Educational Aspirations of Private and Government College Students

Variable	Sample size	X^2
Private	350	56.815*
Government	250	23.097*

* Significant at 0.01 level

From the above table it is clear that the association between achievement and educational aspirations in both the samples was significant and positive.

The significant association between achievement and educational aspirations was higher in the students studying in private colleges than those studying in government colleges.

The hypothesis that *there is no significant difference in the level of association between achievement and educational aspirations of the students of private and government junior colleges* can be rejected.

HYPOTHESIS 3C: There is no significant difference in the level of association between achievement and educational aspirations of boys and girls of junior colleges.

To find out the validity of Hypothesis 3C the chi-square values were calculated. They are given below.

Table 17: Association between Achievement and Educational Aspirations of Boys and Girls

Variable	Sample size	X^2
Boys	300	47. 861*
Girls	300	36.635*

* Significant at 0.01 level

The association between achievement and educational aspirations, seen from the table, was positively significant.

The association of achievement and educational aspirations observed in boys was a little bit higher than that of girls.

The hypothesis that *there is no significant difference in the level of association between achievement and educational aspirations in boys and girls of junior colleges* can be rejected.

ACHIEVEMENT AND ADJUSTMENT

The present study was also intended to identify the association between achievement and adjustment. The chi-square test of independence was applied to identify the association of these two areas. The values and their results are as follows.

HYPOTHESIS 4: **There will be a significant positive association between achievement and adjustment of junior college students.**

Chi-square values were computed to test the validity of the above hypothesis.

Table 18: Association between Achievement and Adjustment in the Whole Sample

Sample	Sample size	X^2
Whole	600	39.235*

*Significant at 0.01 level

The chi-square value states that there was a significant positive association between achievement and adjustment of the students studying in junior colleges.

The hypothesis that *there will be a significant positive association between achievement and educational aspirations of junior colleges* can be accepted.

HYPOTHESIS 4A: There is no significant difference in the level of association between achievement and adjustment of the students of residential and non-residential junior colleges

The above Hypothesis 4A was tested for its validity by using chi-square test.

Table 19: Association between Achievement and Adjustment of Residential and Non-Residential College Students

Variables	Sample Size	X^2
Residential	300	18.428*
Non-Residential	300	31.184*

* Significant at 0.01 level

It is evident from the above table that the association between achievement and adjustment of the students studying in residential and non-residential junior colleges was positively significant.

It also seems from the above chi-square values that there exists a difference in the level of association between achievement and adjustment in residential and non-residential junior college students.

The hypothesis that *there is no significant difference in the level of association between achievement and adjustment of the students of residential and non-residential junior colleges* can be rejected.

HYPOTHESIS 4B: There is no significant difference in the level of association between achievement and adjustment of the students of private and government junior colleges.

Chi-square values were computed to test the validity of Hypothesis 4B.

Table 20: Association between Achievement and Adjustment of Private and Government College Students

Variable	Sample Size	X^2
Private	350	27.812*
Government	250	12.130*

*Significant at 0.01 level

From table - 20, it seems clear that there was a positive association between achievement and adjustment in the students studying in private and government junior colleges.

There was a significant level of difference in the association between achievement and adjustment of the students studying in private and government junior colleges.

The hypothesis that ***there is a significant difference in the level of association between achievement and adjustment of the students of private and government junior colleges*** **can be rejected.**

HYPOTHESIS 4C: **There is no significant difference in the level of association between achievement and adjustment of boys and girls of junior colleges.**

To test the validity of the Hypothesis 4C, chi-square values were calculated.

Table 21: Association between Achievement and Adjustment of Boys and Girls

Variable	Sample size	X^2
Boys	300	28.843*
Girls	300	7.251*

* Significant at 0.01 level

It seems that there was a significant and positive association between achievement and adjustment in both boys and girls.

There was a difference in the level of significance in the association between achievement and adjustment of boys and girls studying in private and government junior colleges.

The hypothesis that ***there is no significant difference in level of association between achievement and adjustment in boys and girls of junior colleges*** **can be rejected.**

CONCLUSIONS AND DISCUSSION

Education is a human enterprise. It is a process and a kind of activity in relation to human beings. It is a continuous effort to develop all capacities of the child, to control his environments and fulfil his requirements. It is an attempt on the part of adult members of the society to shape the development of coming generation. This development is natural and progressive. It is directed towards desirable goals which are fixed by the society according to individual and social needs. Education is also an integrated growth and this growth leads to enlargement of physical organs and maturity of mental capacities. Every child interacts with his environments. This interaction tends to change towards better capacities.

Education is both a product and a process. As a process it involves the act of learning, and as a product it is what we receive through learning, i.e., the knowledge, the ideas and the techniques. In a broader sense, all experiences and acts that have a formative effect on mind, character or physical activity of an individual are of education. Education is a process, by which society, through schools, colleges, institutions and universities, deliberately transmits its cultural heritage, its accumulated knowledge, values and skills from one generation to the next.

One of the most important outcomes of any educational set-up is the achievement of students. Depending on the level of achievement individuals are characterized as high-achievers, average-achievers and low-achievers. The effectiveness of any educational system is gauged to the extent the students involved in the system achieve, whether it be in congnitive, conative or psycho-motor domain. In general terms achievement refers to the scholastic or academic achievement of the student at the end of an educational programme. To maximize the achievement within a given set-up is the goal of every educationist. Many studies indicate in different samples, that the academic achievement is dependent on variables like set-up of educational institution, its organization; socio-economic status of students, their educational aspirations, and their well-adjusted behaviour.

Educational opportunities, though open to all, do not seem to engage to any reasonable extent the capacities of those who seek to avail them of. An eternal question baffling parents, educators and national planners is why do students of demonstrated ability flop in their academic efforts at school or college examinations ? Academic under-achievement more than academic failure, constitutes a grave problem as it amounts to wastage of human resources which is construed as an irreparable loss to the society, which a developing country like ours can ill afford. Hence, the evaluation of achievement levels is necessary so as to plan the academic avenues.

Educationists concern with the plight of the socially disadvantaged. The social back grounds such as home education, economic position, etc., of an individual decide his future efforts and achievements. The relationship between the socio-economic status and achievement of students will facilitate in drawing suitable measures to enhance the student's achievement.

The fruitful approach to study self-enhancement has been the concept of aspiration level. An individual's aspiration level represents him not only as he is at any particular moment, but also as he would like to be best at some point in future. It is a measure of his intentional disposition, an important element of his long range behaviour. So, it is necessary to have the knowledge of the educational aspiration level of a student, both from educational and from guidance point of view.

Every human being seeks adjustment to various situations. He constantly makes efforts to adjust himself to his surroundings because a wholesome adjustment is essential for leading a happy life and gaining satisfaction. Satisfactory adjustment is characterized by behaviour which is both adaptive and constructive. Better adjustment helps a student to achieve academically better result.

At the time of the appraisal of educational development, when many changes are being witnessed in organization, curricula and teaching techniques, it is pertinent to seek systematic and up-to-date information on the significant correlates of achievement . It was felt appropriate to identify the association of achievement with socio-economic status, educational aspirations and adjustment as they have interdependence and as it was not observed earlier in the +2 students. The present study has resulted in drawing the following conclusions which may be utilized in improving the present state of affairs in academic achievement.

The achievement of Intermediate science and mathmatics students studying in junior colleges was high. The distribution of achievement in Intermediate students was also tended towards high achievement.

Not many studies are available on the achievement of students as an independent study, particularly with the Intermediate students. Bhaskara Rao (1989) found that achievement in biology was average in the secondary school pupils. Rani (1980) found that the academic achievement of under-graduate engineering SC students was significantly lower than that of non-SC students. The study of Aruna (1981) also reported similar results. The result of the present study is contrary to the overall achievement of the Intermediate students.

The factors contributing to this high achievement are many and multifarious. The samples selected were in the socio-economically advanced districts of the state. And the colleges were well equipped with laboratory and library facilities. The staff was experienced and the students were of science and mathmatics who were known for their hard work, aspiring high goals. And most important thing is, there is a stiff competition among the residential and non-residential colleges, and private and government colleges for the admission of students, and of course, for their survival also. If the achievement is not good in residential and private colleges they wouldn't be self-sufficient in their maintenance. So, the administrators and the teachers work efficiently in cooperation to improve the academic achievement of their clientele. Contrary to this, for their survival, the members of the teaching staff of the government colleges are forced to improve the achievement of their students also by effective teaching.

The stiff competition among different categories of colleges, availability of adequate laboratory and library facilities, conducive learning atmosphere, experience and efforts of the teaching community, high educational aspirations of the students, socio-economic status of the locality have contributed for this high achievement in the

Intermediate students. If these conditions are provided in all types of colleges, then there will be no question of chromic under-achievement and all the students will come out through the examinations with flying colours.

The achievement in the residential and non-residential junior colleges was different. The students studying in residential colleges were with high achievement, whereas those studying in non-residential colleges were with average achievement. The distribution of achievement in the sub-samples was also not normal. The concentration of achievement in residential colleges was very high in high achievement group, but it was concentrated in averages achievement group and high in non-residential colleges.

Bhaskara Rao (1989) also found that the pupils of residential schools were superior in achievement to their counter parts. The facilities that are available both in private residential junior colleges and Government residential junior colleges are no where available either in private aided or unaided non-residential colleges or in government non-residential colleges. The facilities such as good libraries, well furnished laboratories, teaching learning strategies, the study habits, time table of the institution, institutional set-up, administrator's capacity, advantages of residential system, rapport between teacher and taught media, expertise and commitment of the teaching community, intelligence and hard work of the student clientele might have helped in achieving a high achievement by the residential college students.

Srinivasa Rao and Subramanyam (1982) identified that among the school factors, accommodation, educational level and experience of teachers, availability of instructional material, books and reading room facilities have influence on reading attainment which is one of the prime factors of achievement. So, as far as possible, the above facilities should be extended to all non-residential colleges.

The achievement of the private and government college students was also with much difference. The achievement of private college students was high, whereas it was average in government colleges. As regards distribution of achievement, the achievement concentration in private colleges was very

high in high achievement group, but it was high in average achievement group in government colleges.

Many people say that the conditions such as laboratory and library, class room climate, organizational set-up in private educational institutions will be good. Desai (1979) and Hirunval observed a positive relationship between classroom climate and pupils academic achievement. Verma (1977) observed that the classes of the privately managed schools had a more learning-conducive climate. Rani (1980) and Shasidhar (1981) also concluded that the academic achievement was influenced by institutional factors. Another important thing is, the quality of teaching in private colleges will also be good as there are better teaching learning facilities.

The most quotable thing for this high achievement is that inferior teaching in private colleges will be questioned immediately without any delay, which is not possible in case of government colleges. The teachers will teach throughout a student's career in private colleges as the teacher works in the same institution for a long period without any transfers, and also he understands the flaws and potentialities of his students. All these factors will play a significant role in promoting achievement, and these may be adopted in government colleges also.

There was also a slight difference in the level of achievement in boys and girls studying in junior colleges, but this was less when compared with the variables - type and management of the colleges. The boys were with high achievement where as the girls were with high-average achievement. The achievement distribution in the sub-samples was also different. The achievement concentration of boys was high in high achievement group, where as it was slightly high in average achievement group in girls. This result states that there was not much influence of sex on achievement.

The findings of Thakur (1972) and Second International Science Study (1988) indicate that the boys were superior to girls in science achievement. Contrary to this the same Second International Science Study stated that girls scored higher than boys in biology in some countries and it also concluded that the differences between boys and girls in science achievement were greater in the physical sciences than in the life sciences.

The result of this study and the contradictory findings of the above mentioned studies indicate that if proper facilities are provided, both boys and girls will achieve equally well.

The association between achievement and socio-economic status was highly and positively significant in Intermediate students studying in junior colleges.

The above result supports the studies of Havighurst (1964), Menon (1973), Anand (1973), Abraham (1974), Basavayya (1971 and 1974), Lalithamma (1975), Prakash Chandra (1975), Homchanduri (1980), Goswami (1978), Goswami (1982), Jain (1981), Tripathi , Siddiqi and Somasundaram.

A positive influence of parent's education on achievement has been observed in the studies of Clark (1927), Austin (1964), Basavayya (1974), Satyanandam (1969), Khanna (1980), Menon (1972), Ojha (1979), Choudhary (1975), and Dave and Dave (1971). A positive association between achievement and parents' occupation was also found in the studies of Bear (1928), Austin (1964), Abraham (1974), Menon (1972), Ojha (1979) and Dave and Dave (1971). Mishra, Das and Padhi (1960) found a correlation between house environment and achievement.

But the finding of this study is contrary to the studies of Reddy (1981), Nemzek, Salunke (1979), Chatterji, Mukherjee and Banerjee (1971), and Desai (1979) who found no relationship between achievement and socio-economic status.

As there is a great influence of socio-economic status on achievement, the parents have to take due care about their socio-economic status. They can improve their socio-economic status by improving their educational qualifications, by that they can get promotions in their employment in order to improve their economic as well as social status. Even they can change their occupation depending on their educational qualifications and also with the available financial resources. They can improve their home environment by showing a lively behaviour with their children and elders.

From the government side also there is a lot to be done to improve the economic status of the students as well as their parents. The parents whose children are in educational institutions should be provided with adequate employment opportunities or work to earn their livelihood in order to avoid the involvement of their children in earning their livelihood. Sufficient amount suitable to meet the educational as well as board and lodging requirements of the students, through scholarships or at least as loans to the needy, should be arranged. The students should also utilize properly the financial resources obtained either from parents or from government. If a student is without any financial problems he can excel in achievement.

The association between achievement and socio-economic status was significant and positive in both residential and non-residential college students. But it was a little bit higher in non-residential college students than that of residential.

No major studies are available to compare this result. As there is association between achievement and socio-economic status of students studying in both residential and non-residential colleges, one has to look into the financial requirements of the students as well as into the improvement of social status by following the earlier discussed procedures.

There was a significant and positive association between achievement and socio-economic status of the students studying in private as well as in government colleges. But, the difference in the level of association in the students of private and government colleges was negligible.

As there is no significant difference in the level of association between achievement and socio-economic status in government and private college students, one can say that the opinion, that the rich people or socio-economically advantageous students study in private colleges, is not true. With this it seems that the students' choice in selecting a college depends on the teaching learning atmosphere of a college. So, the administrators of each and every college has to develop a conducive learning atmosphere in the classrooms irrespective of the availability of infrastructural and teaching learning facilities.

The association between achievement and socio-economic status was positively significant in both boys and girls. The association was very high in boys when compared with girls.

Many people in our Indian society try to educate their male children rather than their female children. This may be due to the expectations kept with the male community or may be due to the customs and traditions of our society. So the males might be from high socio-economic status group when compared with the females. This study indicates that the girls with or without better socio-economic status are doing well in their education.

The association between achievement and educational aspirations was highly and positively significant in Intermediate students.

The result of the present study supports the previous studies of Menon (1972), Gates (1948), Kuppuswamy (1974) and Hussain (1977). At the same time it also contradicts with the studies of Gould and Kaplan (1940), Sears (1940), Holt (1942), Shultz and Ricciuti (1954), Sharma (1979), Muthayya (1962) and Radha (1985).

As the educational aspirations are very closely associated with the achievement of Intermediate students, it is necessary to develop proper educational aspirations in all the students. If the educational aspirations of an individual are high, he will try to achieve those goals.

Aspirations are influenced by factors like - wishes for what individuals want to achieve; personal interests, which influence the areas of aspirations; the experiences with successes strengthening aspirations and failures weakening them; the personality pattern, which influences both the kind and the strength of aspirations; personal values, which determine what aspirations are more important; sex, with boys aspiring higher than girls; socio-economic status, with those of the middle and upper groups aspiring higher than those of lower groups; and racial background, with those of minority group status often aspiring unrealistically high in the form of compensation.

Aspirations are also influenced by the environmental factors such as parental ambitions, which are higher in first-born than later-born children; social expectations, which emphasize that those who are successful in one area can be successful in all areas if they wish; peer pressures to set aspirations in areas important to the peer group; group emphasis on sex appropriateness of aspirations; cultural traditions which hold that all people can achieve anything they wish if they try hard enough; social values, which vary with the area of achievement; mass media, which encourage achievement aspirations; social rewards for high achievement and social neglect or rejection for low achievement; competition which siblings and peers have in the hope of showing one's superiority over them.

What ever the conducive procedures may be, the parents and the teachers have to upgrade the positive educational aspirations in students, but this should not lead to frustration when the students fail to reach the level of aspiration. By promoting educational aspirations, one can improve the achievement of the students as it has an influence on it.

The association between achievement and educational aspirations was positively significant in the students studying in both residential and non-residential colleges. The level of association was double in non-residential college students than that of residential college students.

As there is a positive association between achievement and educational aspirations in both residential and non-residential college students, it is the duty of parents, teachers and even society to upgrade the educational aspirations of the students in order to bring better achievement in students. Even though there is a less association between achievement and educational aspirations in residential colleges than that of non-residential colleges, the achievement of residential college students was higher than that of non-residential colleges. This may be due to the better socio-economic status of the residential college students because most of them come from higher socio-economic status groups as they have to pay high fees in private residential colleges other than those managed by the government.

There was a significant and positive association between achievement and educational aspirations of students studying in private and government colleges. The association was higher in private college students than that of government college students.

As there is an association between achievement and educational aspirations of students studying in private and government colleges, the educational aspirations of the students should be promoted and these will, in return, promote the achievement of the students. The difference in the level of association between achievement and educational aspirations may be due to the attraction of private colleges, and the higher aspirations and achievement of the students studying in them. The government colleges also have to work hard in getting better achievement in order to attract the cream of the student community which will be with higher educational aspirations.

The association between achievement and educational aspirations was significant and positive in boys and girls. But there was a slight difference in the level of association as it was a little bit higher in boys than that of girls.

Menon (1972) has observed a strong association between high achievement and educational aspirations in girls.

The significant positive association observed in the cases of type of college and management of college has been observed in the case of sex also. It is also the duty of parents and teachers to promote the educational aspirations of either sex without any discrimination between the two. The study of Bhaskara Rao reveals that the achievement in girls is equally good with that of boys. So equal opportunities must be given to girls also, of course, the Indian constitution also provides equal opportunities to upgrade women's education. The slight difference in the level of association that has been observed may be due to socio-economic status, cultural traditions and taboos, social values, and personal interests. But it is our duty to promote educational aspirations in either sex equally.

The association between achievement and adjustment was highly and positively significant in Intermediate students.

Association was also observed between achievement and adjustment by Nagpal (1979), Abraham (1974), Reddy (1974), Soman (1977), Vashistha (1991), Salunke (1979), Berger and Sutker (1956), Brown (1953), Wellington (1965), Graff (1957), Scott (1958) , Dhami (1974), Goswami (1978) and Assum and Levy (1947).

Congdon (1943), Houston and Marzolf (1944) , Hibler and Larson (1944) and Caroll and Jones (1944) have found several adjustment problems associated with under achievement.

Anderson (1951) observed that many under-achievers were not beset with serious personal problems.

As there is a positive association between achievement and adjustment it is necessary to take up steps to improve the adjustment of students as it is the process by which an individual maintains a balance between his needs and circumstances. The efforts of the individual to adapt himself to the environment, to overcome frustration in achieving the gratification of his needs, may be called the adjustment process. The situation that offers few barriers to the individual will be favourable and aids adjustment. An adjusted individual knows his own strength and limitations, respects himself and others, satisfies his basic needs, shows flexibility in behaviour, and most important, aspires reasonably. Stranswold and Wren (1948) feel that a well-adjusted student in a school/college exhibits his intrinsic interest in the subject which ultimately leads to better achievement.

The adjustment is closely associated with the factors such as family, peer group, society, culture, religion, attitudes, aptitudes, abilities, and educational institutions. The parents have to make the students adjust well and the teachers have to create a democratic atmosphere in the classrooms. Several investigators are of the opinion that academic adjustment or adjustment to the college is an important factor in academic achievement. Students in general and under-achievers in particular have frequently reported problems of adjustment in colleges. Carson (1927) observed that on entering the college the freshman faces a number of new adjustment problems for which he is unprepared. Hence, Stogdill (1929), Angell (1930) and Philips (1930) emphasized the responsibility of the college to help solve student's problems. So, it is the responsibility of the parents, teachers and society to develop a suitable adjustment behavior in the students in order to get higher achievement.

There was a significant and positive association between achievement and adjustment in the students of residential and non-residential junior colleges. The association was higher in non-residential college students than that of residential college students.

Here, in the residential and non-residential college students, a positive association between achievement and adjustment is prevalent. It was observed by Salunke (1979) that educational facilities and emotional happiness at home contributed positively to academic achievement. Hence, the teachers and the parents have to create adjustable atmosphere and they should also try to keep the students devoid of frustrations keeping the idea of higher achievement in view.

The association between achievement and adjustment was also positive and significant in the students of private and government junior colleges. The significance was high in private college students, but it was relatively less in government college students.

Steinzer (1944), Cattell (1945) and Thompson (1948) pointed out that over-achievers were characterized by good adjustment to school and greater awareness and responsiveness to environmental influence. Frankel (1960) found over-achievers conforming to school regulations adjusted better to the academic situation. Christenson (1956), Popham and Moore (1960) and Roberts (1962) observed over-achievers differed significantly from under-achievers in their adjustment to college. French (1958) considers that lack of adjustment to college life in the freshman introduces extraneous influences on scholastic success. Johnson (1947) also held that poor performance in college was due to unsatisfactory adjustment to college. Wig and Nagpal (1972) found that the failure groups had poor adjustment at school and college but not at university. With the above observations it seems clear that the adjustment in an institution also plays a major role in achievement. If a student joins in a college on his own interest and will, whether a private or government with good environment, he adjusts himself well in that educational set-up and achieves well in academic affairs.

The association between achievement and adjustment in boys and girls was positively significant. But, the significance was very high in boys.

The well adjusted of either sex can achieve equally well as there is a positive significance in the association between achievement and adjustment. The high significance in the boys may be due to their higher adjustment as they move freely in the society, college, etc., and also due to their high aspirations or past performances. If the girls do not struggle with the traditions and customs of the society, they can also adjust well and there will be a great association between achievement and adjustment in girls too. It is the duty of the parents to permit their girls at least to enjoy their psychological needs. One should not worry about the women's liberty and allied aspects. If all, either sex, are well adjusted there will be no misunderstandings, no maladjustment, no broken families, and also no chromic under-achievement. So, due importance should be given to the adjustment problems of both boys and girls equally.

SUGGESTIONS FOR FURTHER RESEARCH

This study brings to light some new areas to be studied by the future researchers. The areas and variables which are not covered by this study may be put to test to enlighten the other factors associated with the achievement and the association between achievement and other psycho-sociological variables. Hence, the researchers may think of the following areas to study in detail.

1. Studies on achievement may be extended to other educational levels, viz., primary, secondary, degree, post-graduation, at district as well as state level.
2. Studies on achievement in independent subjects may also be taken up.
3. Studies may be taken up to find out the effect of independent variables on dependent variables in the cases of controlled and experimental groups as this study has not used any controlled groups and variables.
4. Studies may be conducted on achievement to identify its association with other psychological variables in order to enhance the achievement.
5. Studies may be carried out to find out the effect of environmental factors on achievement and its associated variables.
6. Studies may be conducted to find out the influence of locale of the institution, medium of instruction on achievement.
7. Studies may be taken up on the role of psychological variables of teachers in enhancing the achievement.

BIBLIOGRAPHY

Abraham, M. (1974). **Some Factors relating to Under - achievement in English of Secondary School Pupils.** Ph.D. Thesis. Trivandrum : Kerala University.

Alpern, Moris L. (1946). "The Ability to Test Hypotheses". **Science Education.** 30 : 220 - 229.

Anand, C.L. (1973). **A Study of the Effect of Socio - Economic Environment and Medium of Instruction on the Mental Abilities and the Academic Achievement of Children in Mysore State.** Ph.D. Thesis. Mysore : Mysore University.

Anand, C.L. and M.S. Padma (1987) "Correlates of Achievement : A Trend Report" in Buch, M.B., chief ed. **Third Survey of Educational Research.** New Delhi : NCERT.

Anderson, B. and P.A. Spencer (1963), "Personal adjustment and academic predictability among college freshmen". **Journal of Applied Psychology.** 43 : 97 - 100.

Angell, R.C. (1930). **A Study in Under-graduate Adjustment.** Chicago : University of Chicago.

Angelino, H. and R.L. Hall (1960). "Temperamental factors in high and low achieving school seniors". **Psychological Reports.** 7 : 518.

Assum, A.L. and S.J. Levy (1947). "A comparative study of the academic ability and achievement of two groups of college students". **Journal of Educational Psychology.** 38 : 307 - 310.

Bear, R.M. (1928). " Factors Affecting the Success of College Freshmen". **Journal of Applied Psychology.** 21 : 517 - 523.

Berger, I.L. and A.R. Sutker (1956). "The Relationship of Emotional Adjustment and Intellectual Capacity to Academic

Achievement in Introductory Psychology". **Mental Hygiene.** 40 : 65 - 67.

Best, John W. (1982). **Research in Education**, 4th ed. New Delhi : Prentice Hall of India Pvt. Ltd.

Bhaduri, S.S. (1971). **A Comparative Study of Certain Psychological Characteristics of Over- and the Under-achievers in Higher Secondary Schools.** Ph.D. Thesis. Calcutta : Calcutta University.

Bhagia, N.M. (1967). **Directory for Administration and Scoring. The School Adjustment Inventory.** New Delhi : Manasayan.

Bhaskara Rao, Digumarti (1989). **A Comparative Study of Scientific Attitude, Scientific Aptitude and Achievement in Biology at Secondary School Level.** Ph.D. Thesis. Osmania University, Hyderabad.

Bhaskara Rao, Digumarti (1989). **Dhrusya-sravana Bodhanopakaranamulu** (Audio Visual Teaching Aids). Guntur : Nagarjuna Publishers.

Bhaskara Rao, Digumarti (1993). **Jeevasashtra Bodhana** (Teaching of Biology). Guntur : Nagarjuna Publishers.

Bhaskara Rao, Digumarti (1984). "Private Educational Institutions". **The Educational Review** XC : 34-36.

Bhaskara Rao, Digumarti (1989, June 24). 'Private Residential Collegeelu Avasarame !'. **Andhra Patrika** , 5.

Bhaskara Rao, Digumarti (1989, June 25). 'Private Residential Collegeelu Avasarame !'. **Andhra Patrika** , 4.

Bhaskara Rao, Digumarti (1994). **Scientific Attitude.** New Delhi : Sterling Publishers Pvt. Ltd.

Bhaskara Rao, Digumarti (1993). **Vignanasashtra Bodhana** (Teaching of Science). Guntur: Nagarjuna Publishers.

Bhaskara Rao, D., G. Sundara Rao and L. Rathaiah (1988, September 27). "The science teacher has a definite role". **The Hindu** , 19.

Bhat, R.N. and J. Indiresan (1981). **The Correlation of Performance of Students in High Schools with their Achievement in Polytechnics.** Madras : Technical Teachers Training Institute.

Bhatia, K.K. (1991). **Measurement and Evaluation in Education.** Ludhiana : Prakash Brothers.

Biswas, A. and J.C. Aggarwal (1987). **Encyclopedic Dictionary and Directory of Education**, Vol. I. New Delhi : The Academic Publishers (India).

Biswas, A. and S.P. Agrawal (1986). **Development of Education in India**. New Delhi: Concept Publishing Co.

Brandwein, Paul F., Fletcher G. Watson and Paul B. Blackwood (1958). **A Book of Research Methods.** New York : Harcourt, Brace World, Inc.

Brown, W.F. (1953). "The Problems of Probation and Honours Students". **Educational Research Bulletin.** XP : 14 - 16.

Bryan, J.F. and E.A. Locke (1967). 'Goal setting as a Measure of Increasing Motivation', **Journal of Applied Psychology** 51 : 274 - 277.

Buch, M.B., chief editor (1987). **Third Survey of Research in Education, 1979-1983.** New Delhi : National Council of Educational Research and Training.

Buch, M.B., editor (1979). **Second Survey of Research in Education.** Baroda : Society for Educational Research and Development.

Carroll, H.A. and H.M. Jones (1944). "Adjustment Problems of College Students". **School and Soceity.** 59 : 270 - 272.

Cattell, R.B. (1945). "Personality Traits associated with Abilities". **Journal of Educational Psychology.** 37 : 475 - 486.

Chatterji, S., M. Mukherjee and S.N. Banarjee (1971). **Effect of Certain Socio-Economic Factors on the Scholastic**

Achievement of the School Children. Calcutta : Psychometric Research and Service Unit, Indian Statistical Institute.

Choudhari, V.P. Jain (1975). **Factors Contributing to Academic Under-achievement.** Ph.D. Thesis. Nagpur : Nagpur University.

Christensen, C.M. (1956). "A note on Borow's Inventory of Academic Adjustment". **Journal of Educational Research.** 50 : 55 - 58.

Chouhan, S.S. (1978). **Advanced Educational Psychology**. New Delhi : Vikas Publishing House Pvt. Ltd.

Clark, E.L. (1927). "Family Background and College Success". **School and Society**. 25 : 237 - 238.

Clark, J.H. (1953). "Grade achievement of female college students in relation to non-intellective factors". **Journal of Social Psychology**. 37 : 275 - 281.

Coleman, James C. (1969). **Abnormal Psychology and Modern Life**. Bombay : D.B. Taraporewala Co. (P) Ltd.

Congdon, N.A. (1943). "The Perplexities of College Freshmen". **Educational and Psychological Measurement**. 3 : 367 - 375.

Corson, H.F. (1927). "Factors in the Development of Psychoses in College Men". **Mental Hygiene**. 11 : 496 - 518.

Darwin, Charles (1859). **The Origin of Species**. London : John Murray.

Dave, P.N. and C.L. Anand (1979). "Correlates of Achievement - A Trend Report". in Buch, M.B., ed. **Second Survey of Research in Education**. Baroda : Society for Educational Research and Development.

Dave, P.N. and J.P. Dave (1971). **Socio-economic Environment as related to the Non-verbal Intelligence of Rank and Failed Students**. Mysore : Regional College of Education.

Desai, D.B. and Ameeta Govind (1979). **Studies in Achievement Motivation.** Baroda: Centre for Advanced Study in Education, M.S. University of Baroda.

Desai, B.D. (1979). **A Study of Classroom Ethos, Pupils' Motivation and Academic Achievement.** Ph.D. Thesis. Baroda : M.S. University.

Dhami, G.S. (1974). **Iulelligence, Emotional Maturity and Socio-Economic Status as Factors Indicative of Success in Scholastic Achievement.** Ph.D. Thesis. Chandigarh : Punjab University.

English, H.B. and A.C. English (1958). **A Comprehensive Dictionary of Psychoanalytical Terms.** London : Longmans.

Fergusan, George A. (1981). **Statistical Analysis in Psychology and Education,** 5th ed. Tokyo: McGraw-Hill International Book Co.

Festinger, Leon and Katz Daniel (1976). **Research Methods in the Behavioural Sciences.** Delhi : Armerind Publishing Co.

Festinger, L. (1942). "Theoretical Interpretation of Shifts in Level of Aspiration". **Psychological Review.** 49 : 235-250.

Frankel, E. (1960). "A Comparative Study of Achieving and Under-achieving High School Boys of High Intellectual Ability". **Journal of Educational Research.** 53 : 172 - 180.

Freeman, Frank S. (1965). **Theory and Practice of Psychological Testing,** 3rd ed. Calcutta : Oxford and IBH Publishing Co.

French, J.M. (1958). "Validation of New Item Types, Against Four Year Academic Criteria". **Journal of Educational Psychology.** 49 : 67 - 76.

French, J.W. (1959). "The relationship of home and school experiences to scores on achievement". **Journal of Educational Psychology.** 50 : 75 - 82.

Gage, N.L. (1966). **Handbook of Research on Teaching** Chicago : Rand McNally & Co.

Garret, Henry E. (1979). **Statistics in Psychology and Education.** Bombay : Peffer and Simons Pvt. Ltd.

Gates, *et.al.* (1948). **Educational Psychology** . New York : The MacMillan Co.

George, E.I. (1966). **A Comparative Study of the Adjustment and Achievement of 10 years and 11 years Schooling in Kerala.** Trivandrum: Dept. of Psychology, Kerala University.

Good, C.V., ed. (1959). **Dictionary of Education.** New York: McGraw Hill Book Co.

Goode, William J. and Paul K. Hatt (1983). **Methods in Social Research.** Tokyo : McGraw Hill International Book Co.

Graff, A . (1957). "Occupational Choice Factors in Normally Achieving and Under-achieving Intellectually Superior Twelfth Grade Boys". **Dissertation Abstracts.** 28, 17: 2207.

Griffiths, G.R. (1945). "The relationship between scholastic achievement and personality adjustement of men college students". **Journal of Applied Psychology.** 29 : 360 - 367.

Griffits, C.H. (1926). "The Influence of Family on School Marks". **School and Society.** 24 : 713 - 716.

Goswami, P.K. (1978). **A Study of Self-Concept of Adolescents and its Relationship to Scholastic Achievement and Adjustment.** Ph.D. Thesis. Agra : Agra University.

Goswami, R. (1982) **An Inquiry into Reading Interests of the Pupils of Standards VIII to X in relation to Intelligence, SES and Academic Adjustment.** Ph.D. Thesis. Baroda : M.S. University.

Gravetter, Frederick J. and Larry B. Wallnau (1987). **Statistics for the Behavioural Sciences.** New Delhi: McGraw-Hill Publishing Co. Ltd.

Guilford, J.P. (1987). **Psychometric Methods.** New Delhi : Tata McGraw-Hill Publishing Co. Ltd.

Harton, Paul B. and Chester L. Hunt (1984). **Sociology.** Singapore : McGraw Hill International Book Co.

Hibler, F.W. and A.H. Larson (1944). "Problems of Upper Class Students in a Teacher's College". **Journal of Applied Psychology.** 28 : 246 - 253.

Holt, R.R. (1942). "Level of Aspiration as Ego Defence". **Psychol. Bulletin.** 39 : 457.

Homchandhuri, S. (1980). **An Analytical Study of Correlates of Academic Performance of College Students (Tribal) of Mizoram.** Ph.D. Thesis. Baroda : M.S. University.

Houston, V.M. and S.S. Marzolf (1944). "Faculty use of the Problem Checklist". **Journal of Higher Education.** 15 : 325 - 328.

Hurlock, Elizabeth B. (1978). **Child Development**, 6th ed. Auckland : McGraw-Hill International Book Company.

Hussain, M.Q. (1977). **A Study of Academic Attainment in relation to Level of Aspiration and Anxiety.** Ph.D. Thesis. Aligarh : Aligarh Muslim University.

Jayaswal, Sita Ram (1968). **Techniques and Tests in Psychology and Education.** Lucknow: Prakashan Kendra.

Jain, S.S. (1981). **A Study of the Impact of Reading on the Achievement of Pupils of Class VII in Different School Subjects.** Ph.D. Thesis. Vallabh Vidyanagar : Sardar Patel University.

Jensen, V.H. (1958). "Influenence of Personality Traits on Academic Success". **Guidance Journal.** 36 : 497 - 500.

Johnson, R.C. (1947). "The Intellectual Growth of Virginia State College Students". **Virginia State College Gazette.** 53 : 51 - 61.

Jucknat; M. (1937). "Performance, Level of Aspiration and Self Consciousness". **Psychol. Forsch.** 22 : 89 - 179.

Kaur, Gursharan (1989). **Underachievement : Identification Diagnosis and Treatment.** New Delhi: Commonwealth Publishers.

Kerlinger, Fred N. (1964). **Foundations of Behavioural Research.** Holt, Rinehart & Winston.

Khanna, M. (1980). **A Study of the Relationship between students' Socio-economic Background and their Academic Achievement at Junior School Level.** Ph.D. Thesis. Kanpur : Kanpur University.

Kundu, C.L. and D.N. Tutoo (1985). **Educational Psychology.** New Delhi : Sterling Publishers Pvt. Ltd.

Kuppuswamy, B. (1980). **An Introduction to Social Psychology.** New Delhi : Asia Publishing House (P) Ltd.

Kuppuswamy, B. (1974) **A Textbook of Child Behaviour and Development.** Delhi : Vikas Publishing House.

Lalithamma, K.N. (1975). **Some Factors Affecting Achievement of Secondary School Pupils in Mathematics.** Ph.D. Thesis. Trivandrum : Kerala University.

Liebert, Robert M., Rita Wicks Poulos and Gloria Strauss Marmor (1979). **Developmental Psychology**, 2nd ed. New Delhi: Prentice-Hall of India Pvt. Ltd.

Lowel, E.K. and J.W. Atkinson (1953). "The Effect of Need for Achievement on Learning and Speed of Performance". **Journal of Psychology.** 33 : 31-40.

Madesen, I.N. (1930). **Educational Measurement in Elementary Grades.** Yonkers on Hudson : World Book Co.

Malla Reddy, M. (1988). **Student Unrest - A Socio-Psychological Study.** Hyderabad : Department of Education, Osmania University.

Mangal, S.K. (1991). **Educational Psychology**. Ludhiana: Prakash Borthers.

Martin, G.C. (1952). "Interviewing the Failing Students". **Journal of Educational Research**. 40 : 53 - 60.

Menon, S.K. (1973). **A Comparative Study of the Personality Characteristics of Over-achievers and Under-achievers of High Ability**. Ph.D. Thesis. Trivandrum : Kerala University.

Morgan, Clifford T., Richard A. King, John R. Weisz and John Schopler (1986). **Introduction to Psychology**, 7th ed. New York : McGraw-Hill Book Co.

Morgan, H.H. (1952). "A psychometric comparison of achieving and non-achieving college students of high ability". **Journal of Counselling Psychology**. 16 : 292 - 298.

Mathis, B.C., J.W. Cotton and L. Sechrest (1970). **Psychological Foundations of Education**. New York : Academic Press.

Muthayya, B.C. (1962). 'Level of Aspiration and Intelligence of High Achievers and Low Achievers in Scholastic Field', **Journal of Psychological Research.** 9 : 3.

Nagpal, R. (1979). **A Study of Non-intellectual Characteristics of Over- and Under-achieving Engineering Students**. Ph.D. Thesis. New Delhi : Indian Institute Technology.

Narayana Rao, S. (1990). **Educational Psychology**. New Delhi : Wiley Eastern Limited.

Nemzek, C.L. (1940). "The Value of Certain Non-intellectual Factors for Direct and Differential Prediction of Academic Success". **Journal of Social Psychology.** 12 : 12 - 20.

Ojha, K.P. (1979). **A Study of Correlationship between Socio-Economic Status and Achievement of High School Boys.** Ph.D. Thesis. Gorakhpur : Gorakhpur University.

Pal, G. (1982). **An Enquiry into the Factors involved in the learning of Science by Adolescent Pupils.** Ph.D. Thesis. Calcutta : Calcutta University.

Parameswaran, E.G. and C. Beena (1988). **Invitation to Psychology**. New Delhi : Tata McGraw-Hill Publishing Co. Ltd.

Pearl, Richard E. (1974). "The Present Status of Scientific Attitude Measurement : History, Theory and Availability of Measurement". **School Science and Mathematics.** LXXIV: 375-381.

Philips, D.E. (1930). "Mental Dangers among College Students". **Journal of Abnormal and Social Psychology.** 25 : 3 - 13.

Popham, W.J. and M.R. Moore (1960). "A note on the validity of Borow's College Inventory of Academic Adjustment". **Journal of Educational Research.** 54 : 115 - 117.

Ramkumar, V. (1972) . "An Investigation into the Relationship of size of Family to Self-concept and Academic Achievement". **Educational and Psychological Review.** XII : 107-113.

Ramkumar, V. (1972). "Self - Concept and Level of Aspiration as Factors affecting Academic Achievement". **Journal of Psychological Research.** 16 : 139 - 142.

Rani, B. (1980). **Self-Concept and Other Non-cognitive Factors affecting the Academic Achievement of the Schedule Caste Students in Institutions for Higher Technical Education.** Ph.D. Thesis. Delhi : Jawaharlal Nehru University.

Rastogi, K.G. (1983). **Educational Psychology**. Meerut : Rastogi Publications.

Rathaiah, L. and D. Bhaskara Rao (1990). "Residential colleges : relevance in the present system". **The Hindu** : 18.

Rathaiah, L. and D. Bhaskara Rao (1990). "Role of residential colleges". **Indian Express** : 7.

Rathaiah, L. and D. Bhaskara Rao (1990). "Residential Collegeelu Vidyarthulni Aakarshinchadaniki Karanalemity". **Udayam** .

Reddy, C.A. (1981). **Inter-relationship between Organizational Climate of Secondary Schools, Socio-Economic Status of Students, Students' Perception of Rewarding Behaviour and their Academic Achievement.** Ph.D. Thesis. Hyderabad : Osmania University.

Reddy, I.V.R. (1974). **Academic Adjustment in relation to Scholastic Achievement of Secondary School Pupils - A Longitudinal Study.** Ph.D. Thesis. Tirupati : S.V. University.

Roberts, H.E. (1962). "Factors affecting the Achievement and Under-Achievement of Bright High School Students". **Journal of Educational Research.** 56 : 175 - 183.

Rotter, J.B. (1943). "Level of Aspiration as a Method of Studying Personality : III Group Validity Studies". **Character and Personality** . 11 : 254 - 274.

Rummel, J. Francis (1958). **An Introduction to Research Procedures in Education.** New York : Harper and Brothers.

Salunke, R.B. (1979). **A Study of the Home Environment, Socio-Economic Status and Economic Management in relation to the Academic Achievement of the First Year College Students of M.S. University.** Ph.D. Thesis. Baroda : M.S. University.

Saun, G.S. (1980). **Patterns of Self-disclosure and Adjustment among High and Low-achievers.** Ph.D. Thesis. Naintal :Kumaun University.

Saxena, S.K. (1989). **Manual for Educational Aspiration Scale.** Agra : Agra Psychological Research Cell.

Sears, P.S. (1940). "Level of Aspiration in Academically Successful and Unsuccessful Children". **Journal of Abnormal and Social Psychology.** 35 : 498 - 536.

Shah, Beena. (1986). **Manual for Socio-Economic Status Scale.** Agra : Agra Psychological Research Cell.

Sharma, B.A.V., D.R. Prasad and P. Satyanarayana, editors (1989). **Research Methods in Social Sciences.** New Delhi: Sterling Publishers Private Limited.

Sharma, Lalita (1989). **Manual for Indian Adaptation of Bell's Adjustment Inventory.** Agra : Agra Psychological Research Association.

Sharma, Radha R. (1985). **Enhancing Academic Achievement - Role of Some Personality Factors.** New Delhi: Concept Publishing Co.

Sharma, R.R. (1979). **Self-concept, Level of Aspiration and Mental Health as Factors in Academic Achievement.** Ph.D. Thesis. Banaras : Banaras Hindu University.

Shasidhar, B. (1981). **A Study of the Relationship between a few School variables and the Achievement of Schedule Caste Students studying in Secondary Schools of Karnataka.** Ph.D. Thesis. Bangalore : Bangalore University.

Shuttleworth, F.K. (1927). "The Measurement of the Character and Environment Factors involved in Scholastic Success". **University of Iowa Studies Studies in Character.** 1,2 : 80.

Sinha, D.N. (1970). **Academic Achievers and Non -Achivers : An Analysis of Some Factors Associated with Success and Failure in University Education.** Allahabad : University Publishers.

Smith, Edward W., Stanely W. Krouse and Mark M. Atkinson (1969). **The Educator's Encyclopedia.** New Jersy : Prentice Hall.

Somasundaram, M. (1980). **A Comparative Study of Certain Personality Variables related to Over-, Normal- and Under - achievement in Secondary School Mathematics.** Ph.D. Thesis. Calicut : Calicut University.

Srinivasa Rao, R. and S. Subramanyam (1982). **An Intensive Study of Certain Factors influencing the Reading Attainment of Primary School Children**. Tirupati : Dept of Education, S.V. University.

Srivastava, N. (1980). **Intelligence, Interest, Adjustment and Family Status as Predictors of Educational Attainment of High School Students**. Ph.D. Thesis. Gorakhpur : Gorakhpur University.

Steinzer, B. (1944). "Rorchach Responses of Achieving and Non-achieving Students of High Ability". **American Journal of Orthopsychist**. 14 : 494 - 504.

Stogdill, E.L. (1929). "The Maladjusted College Student". **Journal of Applied Psychology**. 13 : 440 - 450.

Stromswold, S.A. and C.G. Wrenn (1948). "Counselling Students towards School Adjustment". **Educational and Psychological Measurement**. 8 : 57-63.

Sudame, G.R. (1973). **A Study of the Effect of Library Use on Academic Achievement of Post - Graduate Students in the M.S. University of Baroda**. Ph.D. Thesis. Baroda : M.S. University.

Taneja, V.R. (1989). **Educational Thought and Practice.** New Delhi : Sterling Publishers Pvt. Ltd.

Taylor, R.G. (1964). "Personality Traits and Discrepant Achievement". **Journal of Counselling Psychology**. 11 : 76 - 82.

Thakur, R.S. (1972). **A Study of the Scholastic Achievement of Secondary School Pupils in Bihar**. D.Litt. Thesis. Patna : Bihar University.

Thompson, G.M. (1948). "College Grades and Group Rorschach". **Journal of Applied Psychology**. 32 : 398 - 407.

Tripathi, B.K. (1978). **A Study of the Relationship between Personality Factors and Social Acceptance, Classroom**

Behaviour and Academic Achievement. Ph.D. Thesis. Jaipur : Rajasthan University.

Vashishta, K.K. (1991). "A Comparative Study of the Adjustment of High and Low Achieving Indian Pupils at Higher Secondary Level". **Journal of Educational Research and Extension.** 27 : 181 - 191.

Verma, R.P.S. (1977). **A Study of School Learning as a Function of Socio-Emotional Climate of the Class**. Ph.D. Thesis. Jaipur : Rajasthan University.

Vignan's Prospectus, 1990-91. Vadlamudi : Vignan Residential College.

Walberg, Herbert J. and Geneva D. Haertel, editors. (1990). **The International Encyclopedia of Educational Evaluation** . Oxford : Pergamon Press.

Wig, N.N. and R.N. Nagpal (1972). **Mental Health and Academic Achievement - A Comparison of Successful and Failed Students**. Chandigarh : Post-graduate Medical Research Institute.

INDEX

NOTES